"For Executives Only is a must for every executive's reading list!"

Read What People Have to Say About *For Executives Only*, The Five O'Clock Club, and Bill and Hélené.

For Executives Only lays out a practical, actionable, no nonsense approach to preparation, delivery and follow-through of the key components of a job search. There can be no doubt that investing time and energy in the full use of this methodology – from self assessment through negotiating and preparing to start a new job – will help any executive make the next move easier, faster and better.

—George Bradt, Managing Director and CEO, Prime Genesis.

I recommend the Five O'Clock Club methodology for executives who want straightforward, practical, user-friendly tools that will help them land not just any job, but one they will truly enjoy, and that is perfect for the career stage they happen to be in.

—Eileen Broer, Founder, The Human Dimension,
Former VP HR Manhattan Life Insurance Company

I had only a few years until retirement and was shocked and quite fearful that I was too old to find *any* job in such a challenging market. Thanks to the Five O'Clock Club outplacement program, I now manage over 50 IT consultants and 6 project managers.

—Joseph Maisto, Director and Senior Manager,
High-growth IT consulting company

When my employment ended, I had great concerns. I had not interviewed for a job in the 8 years that I was there, and I had very diverse interests, an eclectic background, and questions about what would be the best fit for me. The Five O'Clock method, my Five O'Clock coach, and group proved invaluable to me. I continued to work with my coach to help me adapt to a new boss. I frequently recommend the Club to my friends. It works!

—Alan Cohen, Director of Communications,
The League of American Theatres and Producers, Inc.

Thomas Edison claimed that success is 90% perspiration and 10% inspiration, and this is probably true of job search as well. Your analyses will help people be more organized and productive.

—Richard Bond, CEO, Bond & Company

For Executives Only is a very strong book that keeps its promises. I truly enjoyed the conversational style of writing. It's packed with examples, it is easy to read, and also easy to learn from the experiences of others.

—Mark Hurwich, Vice President, Professional Services, Marketrx

For Executives Only is a highly readable book. It's a great way to be reminded about what makes the Five O'Clock process so successful for executives.

—Cynthia Russel, President, Connecticut Housing Investment Fund

For Executives Only is filled with practical applications that illustrate the value of the Five O'Clock Club search methodology. One step that profoundly impacted my search was reaching out to a career coach. The coach held me accountable for producing excellent marketing materials and for asking the tough questions of potential employers. As you apply these principles, your search will be more focused and effective.

—Robert Wood, EVP and COO, John H. Myers & Son

For Executives Only teaches you how to proactively manage your future. Most job searches are *reactive*. *For Executives Only* helps you get *ahead* of the curve, understand when changes are being contemplated in your organization, and then execute an effective job search. It describes the winning formula for achieving an effective job search. *For Executives Only* is a *must* for every executive's reading list!

—William Dumont, VP, World Wide Sales, Orative

There is so much to like in *For Executives Only*. It not only tells you *what* and shows you *how*, but also tells you why.

—Dave Opton, Founder, ExecuNet

I got more value in two hours with my Five O'Clock Club executive coach than I did from the weeks I spent at a major outplacement firm.

—Joe Vetrano, CIO

Bill has an easy-going approach and a sense of humor that helps ease you through the painful process of examining your background, writing a résumé, and focusing your search. Perhaps even more importantly, he is committed to "customer service." Even after the formal part of our process was finished, I still found him incredibly responsive to phone calls and e-mails as my job search progressed. I know he's always in my corner.

—Jill Campbell, Marketing

Hélène makes you leave your comfort zone. With tact, mastery and powerful questioning, she challenged me, and helped me consider my choices and put me on the right career track.

—Gilles T., founder and CEO of a start up

Working with Hélène helped me get back in touch with my leadership strengths. Using her as a sounding board, I was able to step back and make the right decisions for my company.

—Yves H., Executive Vice President, Professional Services

Thank you coach! You are the best.

—Russ Ackerman, Director of Marketing

Hélène offers a disciplined process, and a framework to conduct productive "homework" during the job search. She is not afraid of being honest when you veer off track.

—Dan S., Managing Director, High Tech

As a result of my work with Bill, my résumé became clearer and more powerful. Within four weeks, I landed the executive position that I was seeking.

—Bob Schwartz, Director of Global Marketing

Hélène quickly got me focused on the big picture and then guided me in putting together a coherent plan to go about my job search.

—Geoffrey K., Senior Manager, Pharmaceuticals

Bill has the capacity to help people think clearly and focus on effective strategies. His upbeat attitude was invaluable.

—Jim Baldino, VP Sales

Hélène was instrumental in helping me create a successful exit strategy. She held me accountable and kept me focused as I was designing my next career step.

—Kirsten D., Vice President, Investment Banking

Bill is honest, kind, straightforward, has a great sense of humor, and he knows his business.

—Beth Fitz Gibbon, VP Sales and Marketing

Hélène's insights were a perfect wake-up call. She gave me the external perspective, and the solid framework that I needed to negotiate the best career path at my current company.

—Ambroise W., Director Business Development, Retail

Successfully managing my career search in today's difficult market was a daunting task. Working with Bill was a rewarding experience. He was focused, very accessible and responsive to my needs.

—Sven Saller, VP Sales

Hélène's systematic approach to networking enabled me to quickly become an insider in my target industry and then land the dream job.

—Jean-François P., Managing Director, Private Equity

I got a terrific value for the money.

—Randy Cox, VP Operations

Your straightforward style cuts to the essentials, yet is completely non-threatening. I found it very refreshing and useful.

—Marshall P., Director, Pharmaceuticals

FOR EXECUTIVES ONLY

APPLYING BUSINESS TECHNIQUES TO YOUR JOB SEARCH

BILL BELKNAP and HÉLÈNE SEILER

With a Foreword by Kate Wendleton

Five O'Clock Books
www.FiveOClockClub.com

The
Five
O'Clock
Club®

Executives Only: Applying Business Techniques to Your Job Search by Bill Belknap and Hélène Seiler

1 2 3 4 5 09 08 07 06
Five O'Clock Books is a part of The Five O'Clock Club, Inc.
For more information contact Five O'Clock Books,
300 East 40th Street, New York, NY 10016
Or find us on the World Wide Web at
www.FiveOClockClub.com

For information, please contact:
The Five O'Clock Club®
300 East 40th Street
New York, New York 10016 www.FiveOClockClub.com

Library of Congress Cataloging-in-Publication Data
Seiler, Hélène and Belknap, Bill
For Executives Only: Applying Business Techniques to Your Job Search/by Bill Belknap and Hélène Seiler, with foreword by Kate Wendleton
p. m.
Includes index.
ISBN 978-0-944054-12-3
1. Vocational guidance
2. Job hunting
I. Five O'Clock Club (New York, NY)
II. Title

NOTICE TO THE READER
Publisher does not warrant or guarantee any of the products described herein or perform any independent analysis in connection with any of the product information contained herein. Publisher does not assume, and expressly disclaims, any obligation to obtain and include information other than that provided to it by the manufacturer.

The reader is expressly warned to consider and adopt all safety precautions that might be indicated by the activities herein and to avoid all potential hazards. By following the instructions contained herein, the reader willingly assumes all risks in connection with such instructions.

The Publisher makes no representation or warranties of any kind, including but not limited to, the warranties of ftness for particular purpose or merchantability, nor are any such representations implied with respect to the material set forth herein, and the publisher takes no responsibility with respect to such material. The publisher shall not be liable for any special, consequential, or exemplary damages resulting, in whole or part, from the readers' use of, or reliance upon, this material. The authors and The Five O'Clock Club affirm that the Web site URLs referenced herein were accurate at the time of printing. However, due to the fluid nature of the Internet, we cannot guarantee their accuracy for the life of the edition.

President, The Five O'Clock Club: Kate Wendleton
Chief Operating Officer: Richard C. Bayer, Ph.D.
SVP, Director of the Guild of Career Coaches: David Madison, Ph.D.
Cover Design: Andrew Newman Design
Interior Design and Production: Bookwrights

We dedicate this book to all our wonderful clients.
Without you this journey would not have been possible.

Quotes

A day dawns, quite like other days; in it, a single hour comes, quite like other hours; but in that day and in that hour the chance of a lifetime faces us.
—Maltbie Babcock

One should frame the problem in such a way that a solution is always possible.
—Abel, geometer at the Court of Henri II of France

(On doit donner au problème une forme telle qu'il soit toujours
possible de le résoudre.
—Abel, *géomètre à la Cour d'Henri II*)

If you seek your life purpose, just embrace life, for yourself and for others.
—Simone de Beauvoir, *the Ethics of Ambiguity*

(Si nous n'aimons pas la vie pour notre propre compte et à travers autrui, il est vain de chercher
d'aucune manière à la justifier.
—Simone de Beauvoir, *Pour Une Morale De L'Ambiguïté*)

Enthusiasm *is one of the most powerful engines of success. When you do a thing, do it with all your might. Put your whole soul into it. Stamp it with your own personality. Be active, be energetic, be enthusiastic and faithful, and you will accomplish your objective. Nothing great was ever achieved without enthusiasm.*
—Ralph Waldo Emerson

Table of Contents

Foreword

The original Five O'Clock Club, founded in the 1880's, was one of Philadelphia's famed social clubs. It was made up of 35 leaders of the day, a group that met regularly and formed close bonds. The Club included executives from the Pennsylvania Railroad and Pennsylvania Hospital, the British Consul to Philadelphia and others from politics and the judiciary, shipping magnates and theater moguls, and executives from newspapers and industry.

Today's Five O'Clock Club, started a century later, cultivates the same bonding among members. Forty percent of our Club members earn over $100,000 per year. Almost twenty percent of those earn over $200,000 per year. Members meet privately with their senior coach, and they also meet weekly with their coach and a group of 6 or 7 peers—people at their salary level—primarily via teleconference.

You'll meet the most interesting people in the world at today's Five O'Clock Club—executives from every discipline and industry, and every geographic area in the country. These small groups may include the president of a 1000-person manufacturing company or a major not-for-profit, the international division head of a major entertainment company, VPs and SVPs, C-level executives and managing partners, orchestra conductors and chefs, university executives and city mayors, senior-level controllers and marketers, high-ranking physicians, attorneys and engineers, and the heads of human resources. A group may also include a small-business owner who wants to get back to corporate life, or a corporate executive who want his or her own small business.

Over time, members become "buddies" because, under the guidance of a highly experienced executive coach, they get to know each other well and see each other through an important life change. Many form relationships that last decades. Yes, the Five O'Clock Club still has a social element, but its main focus is business–the business of improving one's career.

The more senior the person, the more likely he or she is to tell the coach: "I'm in your hands. Just tell me what to do." And rightfully so. The Five O'Clock Club has conducted continual career research over the past 25 years, and attracts the best career coaches in the country. Hélène Seiler and Bill Belknap are two of those coaches, and they have written *For Executives Only* as representatives of all Five O'Clock Club executive coaches. You'll need the four basic Five O'Clock Club books covering every detail of the job search, but executives face additional and complex situations. So you need straight talk from Bill and Hélène, advice that only an executive can appreciate.

Five O'Clock Club coaches use a diagnostic approach to determine where a person is in his or her search and what should be done next to move that search along. For example, The Five O'Clock Club developed a way of measuring job-search targets to see whether you have a chance of being successful in your search. Here's an example.

Three executives had worked for the same major publishing company and had been assigned to three different outplacement firms. All three were still unemployed–after a year! One had been the chief financial officer, one was the senior legal counsel and one was the head of MIS–the technology area. I agreed to meet with them as a group to review their searches.

I asked each of them, "How many people have you met with during the past year who are in a position to hire you–that is, people who are more senior than you?" They each admitted to having met very few. Obviously, they were doing something wrong. Now we had to find out *what* was wrong using The Five O'Clock Club's diagnostic methodology.

I selected Jack, the CFO, using him as an example to show all of them the methodology: "Jack, what's the first industry you've been targeting?"

Jack was targeting publishing companies of a certain size, of which there were 13. He said his second target was healthcare, and he was targeting 10 healthcare organizations. Jack had no other targets. He was chasing a total of 23 organizations. Because each organization had only one position that would be right for him, Jack was chasing a grand total of 23 positions. Jack's search was DOOMED from the beginning!

Five O'Clock Club research shows that the average person needs to chase two hundred positions—not 200 openings, but 200 positions to complete their search in a timely basis *and* end in the right job.

Jack now knew he had to expand his search by going after additional industries and additional geographic areas. He immediately began to do that and in fact he got a job within three weeks.

Job hunters can get leads from search firms, ads, networking and direct contact. Jack's lead came from a newspaper ad! He was lucky. The head of MIS got a job within six weeks by doing a targeted mailing. The senior legal counsel relied solely on networking and took considerably longer to find a job.

Our research clearly shows that job hunters get more meetings, for the time spent, through "direct contact" than through any other single technique. Networking (using someone else's name to get a meeting) is important, but very time consuming. You have to find people who are willing to let you use their names. "Direct contact" means aggressively pursuing people whom you may have known in the past or people you may have never met. These might include association members, or people identified on the Internet, through newspaper or magazine articles, or from library research.

We have carefully compared the impact of direct contact and networking. That's what it means to be a "research-based" organization: Finding out what works and letting our members know. Without the research and the methodology, there would be no Club. Hélène and Bill have used Five O'Clock Club methodology and given you their real-life examples of how it applies to senior executives.

And our coaches also help executives throughout their careers—to discuss problems they may have with bosses, peers, subordinates or clients. A Five O'Clock Club coach is often the "secret weapon" behind an executive's success.

That's why you may have heard about us though the *New York Times, Fortune, Black Enterprise, Business Week*, NPR, CNBC, ABC-TV, or other media. They've checked us out and you should too.

Kate Wendleton
President, The Five O'Clock Club
A national career coaching and outplacement organization
www.FiveOClockClub.com

The original Five O'Clock Club was formed in Philadelphia in 1883. It was made up of the leaders of the day, who shared their experiences "in a spirit of fellowship and good humor."

Introduction

In our association with The Five O'Clock Club during the last few years we have coached hundreds of executives through successful job searches. One of us, Hélène (a native of France), coaches clients in the United States and overseas, and the other, Bill, has focused primarily on American clients.

As members of the Five O'Clock Club Guild of coaches, we sometimes meet for training sessions and social events. One afternoon we were discussing some of our coaching successes, as well as some of our—shall we say—more challenging clients. We soon realized there were some amazing similarities: executives tend to view their careers the same way; they face similar challenges when they attempt to change jobs; and there were commonalities in how they *attempted* to run their job-search campaigns. We found these similarities in executives from all over the world.

We also found that, while most of our clients were highly competent in their businesses, nearly all developed a kind of "brain lock" when it came to using all their business skills to find a new job. They didn't seem to realize that the skills they used in preparing for a senior operations review, or for a board presentation, are exactly the same skills needed to prepare for an important interview or networking meeting. Of course, the solution for nearly all of them is the Five O'Clock Club methodology—which we help them to put into practice. Because of our experience with top executives, Kate Wendleton, founder and president of The Five O'Clock Club said, "You guys need to write a book!" We agreed and forged ahead!

So what are the patterns we have found among senior executives?

- First, there was the challenge of getting a good grasp on their career situations.

Many did not know whether their careers were in a "green light, yellow light or red light mode" (a concept you will read about later in this book).

- Executives who are in charge of their careers have a strong 'personal advisory board' made up of past managers and industry experts they respect.
- The *most* successful executives are those who apply to the job search process the same business techniques that brought them to the top. Unfortunately, these are in the minority.
- Those who use a *formal, structured* process do better than those who do not.
- Everyone, from the most successful to the barely successful, have to deal with the "emotional roller coaster" of job search.

So what does this book focus on?

- A proven, research-based job search methodology that is based on more than 25 years of practical experience working with job hunters at The Five O'Clock Club—especially executives who have applied it to their specific situations.
- Actual examples of how our clients have successfully handled:
  - ✦ Doing thorough self-assessment before launching their job search campaigns.
  - ✦ Identifying specific job targets to go after.
  - ✦ Getting their searches off to a fast start.
  - ✦ Marketing themselves.
  - ✦ Networking.
  - ✦ Interviewing.
  - ✦ Dealing with the emotional stress of job search.
  - ✦ Using *proven metrics* to see if their searches are going well.
  - ✦ Negotiating the best compensation packages.
  - ✦ Preparing for starting the new job—and making the adjustment to a different corporate culture.

In comparing notes and stories, we realized that, almost without exception, our executive clients are very quick studies and have a low tolerance for *fluff*. So we knew that this book had to be *to the point* and packed with real-world advice. Executives are, in fact, a perfect market for the very practical, results-oriented Five O'Clock Club methodology.

Client confidentiality, by the way, is our "first commandment." We take it very seriously and even though we mention comparing notes about our clients it is always about their challenges or successes, but never with their real names. For example, if I have a client who has trouble interviewing well by the phone, I can call Hélène and ask how she helped clients with similar challenges. Of course, real names are not used with the client examples given in this book.

One of the most important lessons to learn in the pages that follow is the value of *being proactive*. Don't wait for things to happen: *make them happen*, an approach captured nicely in one of our favorite quotes to keep in mind as you study the chapters that follow:

"If opportunity doesn't knock, build a door." —Milton Berle

Best wishes in your executive job search!

Bill Belknap
Hélène Seiler

1
...

Why This Book?

Chapter Overview ....

- How is the executive job market different?
- A quick test of your market savvy
- What is The Five O'Clock Club methodology?
- Pitfalls to avoid
- Tips on a fast start

....

We had an interesting discussion with an executive about his job search. He and his Board were at odds about the strategic direction of the company so they had decided to "part friends." Several times in his long, successful career he found himself in the job hunt but he told us he never approached it with the same focus or game plan he did when managing a department, division or company. Then he asked, shouldn't I have the equivalent of a Marketing Plan for my search? Or even for my career?

Our response, in a word, was absolutely! And that is what this book is about, bringing The Five O'Clock Club methodology, a proven process, designed over 25 years ago, to your executive job search and your career plan. Just as your well thought out and executed business plan maximizes your success in running a business, so too will your well executed implementation of the methodology maximize the chances of your success in the job market.

Many of our executive clients seem to experience a kind of amnesia when they are focusing on their career or job search. Somehow, they forget that all those wonderful skills they have successfully used to run businesses also apply to running their career. So we will be reminding you throughout the book to link the steps of the process to their equivalent in running a successful business.

For example, all successful companies have a **Marketing Plan** but unfortunately few executives develop a strong marketing plan for their search. The Five O'Clock Club methodology will become your personal marketing plan and, if well developed and well executed, will allow you to run an effective search.

How Is the Executive Job Market Different?

By far the biggest difference is around **expectations**. The expectations prospective employers will have around your skill sets, your knowledge, and your leadership will be extremely high. You know they will not be looking to make many trade offs. You have to bring your "A" Game to the table every time and the tools in this book are designed to help you do that.

Here are some areas we think you should pay attention to because of the potential impact on your career planning and job search.

- **The competition is fierce.** According to National Future Institute Research, 97% of senior executives and managers know someone who is looking for another job, and 40% of those looking are still working. In addition, the average tenure for senior executives keeps dropping. For example one survey of nearly 1,500 executives, conducted by ExecuNet, showed corporate leaders were changing companies every 3.6 years and this number has been dropping annually.
- **The job search process has become increasingly complex.** It is no secret we live in a global economy and the world is getting to be the size of an orange. While most of our clients grasp this intellectually and from their real world experience, few think about the implications for their own career planning or job search.
- **Employers are changing their approach for recruiting senior executives.** Gone are the days when companies just called their favorite retained executive search firm. Although this is still done, they now focus on their own networks, internet résumé banks, and postings on their own website.

Another trend is that companies are working harder to retain their "A" Players and they are working harder to groom them in-house. The proof for us is, we have had a significant number of clients, in the past few years, who have lost the offer to an internal candidate.

- **A quick test of your market savvy.**

The chances are your next potential employer will be probing you during the interview process to assess your savvy on both global and domestic trends.

Do you know the top 3–5 domestic and global trends in your industry?

Are you in touch with the thought leaders in your industry, either personally or through reading?

Are you asked to speak about your industry?

Do you talk with the top executive recruiters to learn how they view current executive hiring criteria in your industry? And what do they feel are the hot topics?

Any "no" answers and you need to bone up . . . quickly!

How To Bring Your "A" Game To Career Planning and Job Search

How many times have you talked with your staff over the years about the need to bring their "A" Game to a particular project or this quarter's revenue targets? A lot, right? And why? Because, just like in the world of sports, we want to win and we want our team to win. Well the same thing is true in the world of career planning and job search. You face just as tough a competitor, in the job market, as you faced fighting your company's competitors. So what does an "A" Game look like in a job search?

We have observed over the years some key qualities and techniques of successful executives in job search. Here is a quick summary. We will discuss each below.

- They tackle **learning the methodology** with the same drive and focus they use to run their department or company.
- Most have **a personal "advisory board"** made up of respected friends and business associates who have been chosen based on their expertise and willingness to give unvarnished feedback.
- Most use a **Career Coach**.
- They all realize the importance of staying on top of their game so they quickly assess the areas where they need to improve. It maybe **their job market savvy**, it maybe interviewing, it maybe networking, it maybe negotiating. Whatever the need they go after it with a vengeance. They also use their Advisory Board and Five O'Clock Coach as part of their assessment and action plan development.

- They all want to know how to **shorten the search** and how to get off to a **fast start**.
- All want to know the **most common mistakes** executives make in their job search.

Let's look at each area in more detail.

Learning the Five O'Clock Club Methodology

Remember your mindset the first time you were asked to make a major presentation to the Board? Remember your first operating plan presentation to the senior staff? You left no stone unturned. Right? You knew every gory detail about the numbers. You thought through every possible question that could be asked. You were totally up-to-date on the competition. You had a contingency plan for that inevitable statement by the CFO, "Mary, you have a great plan but we need you to cut your expense number by 12% and your headcount by 2." You practiced the presentation. **You were totally prepared.** You knew the subject matter cold.

Well, now all you have to do is **the same things for your job search**:

- **Assessing yourself.** The Seven-Stories Exercise and Your Fifteen-Year Vision. Chapter 3
- **Targeting the right job.** Chapter 4
- **Measuring the effectiveness of your search.** Chapter 8
- **Networking.** Chapter 6
- **Your Two-Minute Pitch and your "elevator speech."** Chapter 5
- **Developing a dynamite résumé.** Chapter 5
- **Campaign preparation and management.** Chapters 7, 9 and 11
- **Interviewing and follow up.** Chapter 7
- **Salary negotiation.** Chapter 10
- **Preparing for your first three months on the new job.** Chapter 12

Importance of a Career Coach

"In any game, a player who wants to make it big looks for a good coach to guide, cajole, counsel, encourage, teach, mentor, and explore the possibilities." —J.E. Walker

Many executives spend serious money on fitness coaches, golf coaches, tennis coaches, sailing instruction, or bridge lessons but for some reason hesitate when considering a career coach.

In the spirit of balance we are going to give you **five reasons you don't need a career coach** and five reasons you should seriously consider one.

You Don't Need a Career Coach When . . .

- Everyone loves your résumé.
- Everyone you contact can't wait to talk to you.
- Your biggest challenge in your search is not double-booking appointments.
- You have too many opportunities to pursue them all.
- Your confidence never wavers.

Five reasons you need a Five O'Clock Club (5OCC) Coach

1. A Coach provides immediate expertise.

This is a good news, bad news scenario. The good news is: Many executives have not had to spend much time focusing on a job search. Their networks always seemed to pay off. The bad news is: When faced with that daunting challenge they have little real world experience to draw upon so the *coach* becomes a critical resource for what works and what doesn't.

The average experience level of our executive coaches is over 20 years. Together they have worked with thousands of North American and international executives.

2. They improve the self-assessment phase.

One of the most critical steps in the process is the *self-assessment phase*. There are several tools you will be using including the Seven-Stories Exercise and the Fifteen-Year Vision. (See The Appendices.)

Your *coach* becomes an invaluable asset to guide you through these exercises by helping you synthesize the data and develop logical career targets.

Your *coach* acts like a typical venture capitalist testing the solidity of your strategy, in this case a search strategy and not a product strategy. Your *coach* will work with you to make sure your strategy is strong enough to get you through all the potential pitfalls and speed bumps of your search.

3. They act as a sounding board.

You will find this to be one of the most important benefits of a *coach*. While our clients bring a wealth of practical business knowledge to the job search process they often struggle with keeping their objectivity when approaching an important networking meeting, interview or compensation discussion. A *coach* provides that critical, objective view point and you end up making better decisions on the most important issues.

4. They objectively evaluate the effectiveness of your search.

At The Five O'Clock Club we measure the effectiveness of your search "by the numbers." Sound familiar? We will constantly be asking you "How many Stage-1 contacts do you have? How many Stage 2? And how many Stage 3?" This will be covered in Chapter 8.

The important role the *coach* plays here is giving you practical ideas on how to get the right numbers in each stage.

5. They will pick you up when you are down.

Finding a new job is like riding a roller coaster. You will have incredible highs but you will also have those gut wrenching dips.

An experienced *coach* is sensitive to this dynamic and will be there with practical advice. The advice may range from "stop your search!" (temporarily) and go have some fun, take a long walk, smell the roses, visit a museum, or play with the kids. The *coach* will also constantly remind you of your strengths and tell you, you are twice as good as you are giving yourself credit for. A *coach* will also give you "tough love" when necessary including the directive, "stop surfing the web and get on the phone!"

Here is what a few of our executive clients have said about using a Coach.

"Invaluable. Wish I had started earlier in my career with a coach to help me with the political aspects of my job." —Chief Marketing Officer

"You were the greatest tool for me. You kept me focused, provided a sounding board for strategy and tactics, and I no longer felt isolated." —Communications Executive

"You were my 'working world's' therapist and I liked the fact you could warn me of the stumbling blocks and speed bumps I might encounter during my search." —Wall Street Vice President

"I got more value in two hours than weeks at a major outplacement firm." —Chief Information Officer

"You cannot do it without a good sounding board. It is hard to catch your own mistakes." —Technology Executive

"Although each and every step was considered we picked a customized route. Other coaches would have spent a lot of time on defining what I wanted to do and less time getting me into action. "Go for it" was a frequent phrase that helped me overcome my inclination to have a perfect a plan before taking action. You made me think twice about actions and choices. You told me, "you can do better" when I was thinking of accepting a position with company "X." —Pharmaceutical Executive.

"Same effect as a sports coach. You reminded me constantly of what was at stake and how to improve every step of the way." —Investment Banking Executive

Advisory Board

An Advisory Board is just a fancy way of saying a group of people you trust to give you insight on key subjects and key functional areas like IT, Finance, Human Resources, Sales or Marketing. A strong Advisory Board will help you evaluate opportunities, serve as a sounding board and give you unfiltered feedback. They become, if you will, your "group coach."

We also have a number of clients who have advisors in areas like health, fitness and spiritual needs.

Common Mistakes Executives Make: A Case Study

We want to share with you a typical situation with one of our clients. We will call her Cindy. Five months ago, Cindy, a 50 year old, bi-cultural COO was laid off from a mid-size European company with operations in the US.

Cindy had worked for the company for 10 years, moving up through the ranks from a manager in France to COO in the US operation.

Unfortunately **Cindy's network was limited and scattered** between France, where she grew up, New Hampshire where she had settled, and Alabama where she had gone to school. She seldom returned calls from executive recruiters.

Part of her severance package included outplacement with a large firm. Her plan was to quickly update her résumé so she could start contacting local headhunters. She felt this was all she needed to do. She basically ignored her career counselor's advice to do some career assessment before jumping in and updating her résumé and randomly calling local headhunters. He also recommended Cindy start working on beefing up her network.

Well, ten weeks later Cindy started to panic and for good reason. She had had a few polite conversations with headhunters, but they were not presenting her to their clients. She really did not know what else to do, apart from frantically scanning job ads, which were not producing many more leads.

Why didn't Cindy try what her career counselor had advised? Why was she avoiding career assessment? Cindy had worked in the same industry since graduation, and she had been a successful COO so she wasn't willing to consider any other field.

Then Cindy had a breakthrough. Len, her former boss, was coming to New Hampshire for a convention and gave her a call. Over dinner Cindy told him about her situation. Len commented this was very typical and walked her through the pitfalls he personally had encountered during his own transition. He mentioned that he had worked with the Five O' Clock Club and how, after learning their methodology, totally revamped his approach to his search. He also told Cindy he found his current position in less than 6 months.

Here is the feedback Cindy got from Len.

1. **Do your career assessment** even if you are sure you want to stay in the same industry because everyone needs a plan B.
2. **Your network is too small.** Cindy had only 40 people identified in her network and Len told her she needed several hundred. Something Len learned from our research. (We show you how to expand your network in Chapter 6)
3. **You are not managing your time well**. Cindy was spending valuable daytime hours (3 hours or more) surfing the web and browsing want ads in the newspapers, instead of calling people and lining up meetings.
   (Time management is covered in Chapter 9.)
4. **You need to be better organized.** Cindy did not start the day with a written "to do" list. In fact she had no written plan. This is another one of those "amnesia" areas. The majority of our clients wouldn't think of starting the day, at work, with out a "to do" list but as soon as they are in job search mode the skill seems to evaporate. (Chapter 9)
5. **Start being more persistent** and stop worrying about being perceived as a pest. Cindy was calling 1 or 2 people a day when she should have been calling at least 8! Persistence is everything in a good job search. (In Chapter 6 we will give you some great tips on how to be persistent *without* being a pest.)

Secrets To A Fast Start

Think for a minute what you have done in the past to get a project, reorganization or product out the door ahead of schedule. We bet the first thing you did is to call together all the people who could make it happen and ask them, "How do we pull this off?" Then you probably found someone who could produce a schedule complete with risks and opportunities. You inspired a sense of urgency.

It is not a lot different with launching a **Fast Start** with your search. You must have that same sense of urgency you did back in the office. Here are the key elements of a Fast Start:

- Begin the Self-Assessment Phase (Seven-Stories and Fifteen-Year Vision) immediately, not next week.
- Let all your allies and ex-bosses know your situation as soon as possible.
- Talk to your advisors.
- Hire a Five O'Clock Club coach.
- Set up your home office as "job search central," this means limiting its use for your personal stuff.
- Have a private business line and private email.
- Commit to working 35–40 hours a week on your search.

Chapter Summary ....

Please read this book as though you were going to be tested on it. If you really understand and implement the Five O'Clock Club process . . . you **will be** successful in your search.

2
...

Career Danger Signals:
What To Look For

Chapter Overview . . . .

- Your career traffic signals . . . are they green, yellow or red?
- What to do when your career light changes color.

When you drive your car and approach a traffic light it tells you how to proceed to the intersection. Wouldn't it be nice if there was a "career traffic light?" Good news, we think there is but unfortunately, as we have found, most successful managers are paying so much attention to the tasks at hand they often end up "running their career traffic lights."

- How clearly are you seeing your career danger signals?
- Did you ever get blindsided when your boss said, "we need to make a change"?

Below is a quick guide to reading your personal career traffic light and what to do when you see it change color.

. . . .

Green Light Mode

You will know your career is in the **Green Light** mode if:

- Your career is on track. This means you have written career objectives, including a time line. By the way, studies have shown that people with written career objectives make considerably more income than those who just keep their career objectives in their head.
- You have a good reading on your next one or two moves.
- You have recently been told by your boss or the board, hopefully in writing, you are exceeding their objectives.
- You enjoy your job.
- Your boss has delegated to you things he or she would normally do.
- You are being considered for a significant promotion.
- You are in good health and are satisfied with your work-life balance.

However, Green Lights don't stay green forever. We encourage you to maintain and develop your internal and external networks, volunteer for cross-functional task forces and accept speaking engagements. Do not drop your guard when in Green Light mode and remember, "the best defense is a good offense."

Yellow Light Mode

You know that driving through a **Yellow Light** can get you into trouble but how about at work or at home? Below are situations where you should be prepared to brake. We will also give you some tips on what to do when you see a Yellow Light in the distance.

In our experience two or more of the following mean you are looking at a Yellow Light for your career:

At Work

- You are not clear about your next move. Here we don't mean the exact title but directionally like operations, marketing or finance.
- No one has discussed a long-term career plan with you.
- You haven't had a career discussion with your boss or your boss's boss in the last 12 months.
- You aren't sure whether you fit the culture of the company.

- The company is highly leveraged or has cash flow issues or both!
- The company or Division is not performing in the top quartile of its industry or market.
- A merger, takeover, management buyout or sale of your company. It doesn't matter what side of the deal you are on.
- A re-organization.
- A new boss, even if you know her.
- A change in the relationship with your boss. For example, your review just dropped a rating in one category or several categories.
- Loosing key people on your team or having new team members added without your approval.
- A major new account, client or project has been added to your responsibilities.
- Your mentor or a strong supporter leaves.
- A new position, especially if it requires changes in geography, function, industry, size of business, nature of your team, or amount of travel required.
- You are no longer invited to some key meetings.
- There are persistent rumors about your department.
- You have some key people in the organization who make no secret they disagree with your direction and style.

At Home

- A change in your mental or physical health.
- A change in residence, this can be very deceptive because on the surface it may appear positive but any relocation is high on the stress scale.
- A change in your commute.
- A change in your personal relationships like marriage, divorce, or a new relationship.
- A change in your family life: birth of a child, eldercare, death of a family member or friend.
- A change in your financial obligations: unexpected expenses, remodeling the house, college expenses.

OK, so you have a couple of these situations going on in your life. What should you consider doing besides slamming on the brakes?

- First, take your foot off the gas for a second.
- Don't make any quick decisions.
- Talk with people in the company you respect. Ask them how they perceive your potential. Listen to what they think.
- Have a serious career discussion with your boss and his or her boss.
- Get to know more decision-makers and influencers inside the company especially those outside your functional or operational area.
- Step back and assess exactly what's going on. Is this event having an impact on your work, your attitude or your motivation?
- Are friends or co-workers frequently asking, "is there anything wrong?" "Are you okay?"
- Reach out to your boss, mentors, peers and friends. Ask for feedback if you aren't sure how you are coming across.
- Start listing the resources you may need to address the challenges, include both office resources and family resources.
- Begin strengthening your network.
- Stay visible, speak at conferences and industry organizations.
- Help mentor others.
- Consider professional help: an Executive Coach, a spiritual leader, a psychologist or family counselor.
- If you decide the changes and challenges will lead to a no-win situation then you may decide it is time to leave the company and you begin an aggressive search.
- Make an effort to build bridges to your key detractors. This takes guts but can pay big dividends. The important thing is to understand how much is a perception problem and how much is a strategic or operational difference of opinion.
- Stay current on global trends in your industry and be aware of your "market value." The latter can do wonders for your confidence.
- Work harder to have a more balanced life.
- Protect your health with exercise, proper diet, relaxation and fun! While this is last on our list we think it is **the most important**.

Case Study: How Josh Dealt With His Yellow Lights

Two years ago, we received a call from Josh, a successful general manager of a $1B US subsidiary of a European financial services company. Josh had been with the company for four years and he called because he wanted to know what his "market value" was and he wanted us to provide him with some benchmark data. We first asked why? He said he thought he was underpaid and wanted to look for a similar job but in another company. We agreed to meet and sensed there was something more going on than just a comp issue.

Josh told us that he was working too hard. On paper he was successful, delivering above expectations, but Josh did not have time for anything but work. In his late forties, he was single but was anxious to start a family. He also had been very athletic but could not find the time to exercise. He said his relationship with his European boss was courteous, but distant. He was uncomfortable bringing up the topic of compensation. He had no mentors or sponsors in the company. In addition he was not getting along very well with three of his direct reports who were having performance problems and in fact he had lost his temper with them several times. He also admitted he had a fairly negative attitude.

Obviously Josh is facing a bunch of Yellow Lights! No wonder he wants to leave.

So what did we recommend? First, we discouraged him from leaving prematurely. Then we encouraged him to work on the relationship challenges with his boss and subordinates. We told him a new company would not be tolerant about his temper and in fact would fire him quickly if he has serious relationship issues with new subordinates. Josh agreed and began to prepare a proactive, positive strategy.

He immediately sat down with his direct reports and began to positively coach two of them. The third was not a fit for his area and was transferred.

We also urged him to plan more frequent trips to the European headquarters and other subsidiaries in order to strengthen his relationships with his boss and other key operating people. This turned out to be a gold mine. He re-connected with a former boss and asked him if he would consider becoming a mentor and to his pleasant surprise got agreement.

The ending: After 6 months Josh went back to his boss and put his hat in the ring for a General Manager spot in a much larger business unit. Yes, he got the job and has now been there for over a year.

The story has a wonderful ending but we must put in a quick disclaimer. The ending is a result of Josh executing his plan effectively not because we coaches had the answers. We provided some candid feedback and lots of encouragement but Josh did the heavy lifting.

Another important lesson we can learn from Josh and that is to first look inside your own company!

Experienced marketers are always telling us that increasing the loyalty of existing customers is much more efficient and cost effective than acquiring new customers. The same goes for a job search. We strongly recommend looking first in your own backyard. Explore all the areas in the company. The grass may appear greener on the outside, but it seldom is. It is also a thousand times easier to network effectively and schedule meaningful meetings inside your company than making those dredded cold calls to people you don't know.

Red Light Mode

Red Lights are the easiest to see. We all know we need to stop immediately. A Career Red Light also calls for immediate action.

Let's look at a few of the most common Red Lights and what to do about them.

At Work

- You are fired from your current position.
- Your boss suddenly resigns.
- Your division or company has a series of bad quarters.
- Your position is eliminated and there are no alternative positions.
- Your company has been acquired and they already have "one of you!"
- You just received an "average" performance review or worse.

At Home

- You are unable to continue your job because of an illness.
- You have to resign from your job because of a life-changing situation.

Here are a few ideas from a number of Five O'Clock Club clients who found themselves faced with one of the Red Light situations. You will notice the key pattern, in all three cases, is how proactive and immediate their actions were.

- Mary, an experienced Marketing Director, just learned her company was being acquired by another company who had a major marketing department with an experienced, highly competent Marketing Director. She immediately pulled her family together and described in detail what was going on at work.

She asked for their input and shared her "draft" strategy. There was a lot of give and take but everyone agreed she should immediately begin reaching out to her network and pursue outside opportunities. She also sat down with an old boss and mentor to get his advice.

- Immediately pulling your family together may sound like a no brainer but we often have to take our clients "kicking and screaming" into this step. Yet when you think about it, it is the quickest way to get the family behind you rather than have them wondering why you are so edgy or why you now get home at 5 PM!

- Corey was Director of an Equity Trading Desk at a major bank. The day his boss told him his position had been eliminated, he went back to his office and did three things:

  1. He called home to share the news and put the home renovation project on hold.

  2. He called his major clients to tell them his company had decided to eliminate the Trading Desk and he would be leaving. The good news was, most of his major clients asked him to be sure and tell them where he was going because they wanted him to continue to manage their accounts.

  3. He reached out to all the Directors and VPs he knew at his current competitors and told them the following: the Trading Desk has been eliminated and he would like to explore whether there were any similar opportunities with them. And of course he mentioned what his major clients had told him.

- Jane, the VP of Finance in a large manufacturing company, had just gotten great news: she was having triplets! Unfortunately there were some medical complications that required considerable bed rest early in the pregnancy so she couldn't maintain the pace of her demanding job.

  Within 24 hours of learning about her pregnancy complications she sat down and outlined a proposed transition plan to review with her boss and the SVP of HR. Fortunately she had been developing one of her direct reports, Jeff, who was now considered promotable. Her boss and the SVP of HR agreed with her plan to begin transferring duties to Jeff. They also agreed with her suggestions about her career path once she returned.

Chapter Summary ....

If you are in a Green Light situation:

✓ Leverage your current position and strengthen it.
✓ Be visible and build your internal networks.
✓ Continue to hone your leadership skills.
✓ Get on high visibility task forces.
✓ Keep job, family and your health in balance.
✓ Constantly scan for Yellow and Red Lights.

If you are in a Yellow Light situation:

✓ Don't think that changing companies will solve your problems.
✓ History shows most of our problems "are ours."
✓ If you own your problems, history also shows the chances of you fixing them are excellent.

If the light turns Red:

✓ Be Strategic as well as Tactical.
✓ Start immediately.
✓ Procrastination is guaranteed to bring unhappiness.
✓ Networking is the key.
✓ Reach out quickly and build an advisory board, consider a coach and make your family part of your support system.

....

3
...

Finding the Right Job: *It Is All About Self-Assessment!*

Chapter Overview ....

- Importance of self-assessment . . . key to landing a great job
- Two powerful self assessment tools: The Seven Stories Exercise and Your Fifteen-Year Vision

"Accurate self-assessment lets a leader know when to ask for help and where to focus in cultivating new leadership strengths. Knowing their abilities with accuracy allows leaders to play to their strengths."

—Daniel Goleman, Richard Boyatzis, Annie McKee

....

Self-Assessment Overview

Everyone knows that skills, interests, personality, management style, and values play a critical role in choosing a career. You heard this from high school guidance counselors, again in college and grad school. Perhaps you paid close attention, well, maybe not in high school. Unfortunately, for some of us, our school days were the last time we attempted serious self-assessment.

Now that you are considering making a job change this is the perfect time to do a serious self-assessment for a number of very practical reasons: you will interview better, and it greatly increases your odds of landing the right job with the right team.

Landing a Great Job

Jim Collins, in his book, *"Good to Great"* said, *"Few people attain great lives, in large part because it is just so easy to settle for a good life."*

So here is your challenge: don't settle for a just a "good job." **Plan for a great job!** And to plan for a great job means you must seek work where and how you will perform best.

The first step for landing a great job is self-assessment and for the Five O'Clock Club that means answering several key questions:

- Are you satisfied with where you are?
- Do you have a good handle on your strengths and weaknesses?
- Do you know where you want to be in 5, 10, 15 years? Do you have a written plan to get you there?

We find many executives shy away from self-assessment when they begin their job search even though they would never think of tackling a major problem or opportunity at work without doing rigorous assessment.

The pros and cons of doing a "great" self-assessment:

The Pros

- Recruiters and employers expect you to fully understand yourself.
- Self-assessment confirms strengths, but more importantly **it uncovers strengths you may be taking for granted** and may not be talking about in your interviews or have left off the résumé.
- Assessment reminds us of our weaknesses and allows us to carefully prepare to deal with them in interviews.
- Remember recruiters and employers want leaders who have a clear sense of who they are, warts and all. They also expect you to have a clear vision of the business you are in and your career.

The Cons

Here is what some of our clients have said about the "cons:"

- "This phase is too time consuming."
- "I need to take advantage of this opportunity, fast."
- "This phase might be good for new leaders but I am much too experienced."

Does self-assessment take time? Of course it does, but we are talking hours, not days or weeks.

The Five O'Clock Club Assessment Process

The self-assessment process is a series of exercises to help you better understand yourself and confirm your career plans.

While we use the word "job" **we always mean it in the context of the right career**. So every time you see the word "job," think "career." Your next move **should always** be evaluated based upon how it positions you toward your ultimate career goal.

Most of you, being experienced managers and executives, already have an established career, but it is always good to step back and reflect.

We use several powerful assessment tools:

- **The Seven Stories Exercise.** In this assessment you focus on your proudest accomplishments. From these accomplishments will flow your strongest, most enjoyable, business and personal skill sets. You will assess the direction of your career, focus on any accomplishments you have left off your résumé and prepare compelling stories to use in interviews.
- **The Fifteen-Year Vision.** This is very similar to the Long Range Plan (LRP) you use on the business side except you focus on where **you** want to be in fifteen years versus the business.
- **Your past.** The Five O'Clock Club does not believe it is healthy to spend too much time thinking about the past however you do need to review recent jobs from two perspectives. First, the environments where you excelled then the environments where you may have experienced some speed bumps. Second, a critical review of the peers and managers with whom you worked best and those you didn't. This will begin building the foundation for making good decisions as you evaluate potential opportunities.

The Seven Stories Exercise

"I have never felt so grounded about my strengths. I feel that I am able to better articulate them and match them to my client's needs." —Dan, VP of Key Account Management commenting on The Seven Stories Exercise.

We like Dan's quote because it represents the fundamental theme we hear from all our Five O'Clock Club clients.

Here is how to begin self-assessment. First, make a list of your 20–25 proudest and most enjoyable accomplishments, from all parts of your life, not just successes at work. Here are some areas to look at:

- Your early career.
- Your last few jobs.
- Community or religious work.
- Hobbies.
- Family events.
- Experiences in school, from your earliest school years through college and grad school. One client, for example, picked, as one of her proudest accomplishments that she landed the lead role in a third grade play. She went on to become a company spokeswoman and was outstanding on TV and in radio interviews. So our success roots are often very deep. They also make for great stories to tell in interviews.

As you do this think about those things that gave you a sense of accomplishment and pride. After you list of 20–25, select the seven that are most important to you and write a brief paragraph about each. Once you have completed the paragraph it is time to "peel the onion" using the following questions.

Story #1: Organized my parents 50th Anniversary Party.

What was the main accomplishment for you?

What about it did you enjoy most?

What did you do best?

What was your key motivator?

What led up to your involvement? (Assigned to do it? Self initiated?)

What was your relationship with others? (Leader? Team member? Worked alone?)

What was the environment you performed like?

What was the subject matter? (Product launch? New market? Music? Conservation?)

Story #2: Opened the first sales office in Japan.

(Repeat the same questions for each story)

The time it takes to complete the Seven Stories varies. Most take a few hours, others like to do it over several days focusing first on personal accomplishments then on their business accomplishments.

Case Study: How Lauren Used The Seven Stories To Avoid A Career Road Block

When we started working with Lauren she was a successful VP at a major consulting firm. She realized her career path was blocked, at least on her timetable. There were several, equally successful, SVPs above her with no sign they would be moving for the next few years. So she began to think about other consulting opportunities but she wasn't clear about the type or size of firm she should be targeting.

We suggested she begin to do some self-assessment, starting with the Seven Stories.

Here are four of Lauren's Seven Stories, in her own words, and how she analyzed them. They mix her personal and professional experiences and they allowed her to focus on her strengths, key skills and preferred work environments.

Story 1:

I chose to do my graduate internship in Indonesia and was introduced to the president of a successful local manufacturing company. A few minutes into the conversation, the president told me: "You are a Western business woman and you sound smart. How could you help me? I have a marketing problem in my company."

After 10 intense days of internal audit, I was able to clearly communicate their marketing problem. They had good products but they were not choosing the right kind of markets for growth. I came back with three major ideas to build growth. The president gave the go-ahead on two. I chose a team of English-speaking, entrepreneurial marketing employees and got to work. Four months later, the implementation plans were well under way and were starting to yield tangible results. The day I left, the team members and the president drove me to the airport and everybody cried.

After Lauren reflected on her first story she started to summarize the skills, values and environmental characteristics she saw in the story.

- My underlying skills: entrepreneurship, adaptability, creativity, autonomy, charisma, client orientation, analytics, team leadership.
- My values: independence, adventure, risk taking, recognition, influence.
- Right work environment: entrepreneurial, fast-paced.

Story 2:

After graduation I spent 18 months working for Doctors Without Borders, serving in Tanzania. At the time, I was unsure of my strengths and was searching for who I was. I had a good relationship with the team leader. He praised me for my intelligence, wit and fitness. He even tried to convince me to prepare for a Mt. Everest climb! He helped me focus on my core strengths which led to my decision to start my career in consulting. In fact, he continues to be a strong mentor.

- My underlying skills: self-knowledge, humility, reaching out for help.
- My values: personal growth and development, competition.
- Right work environment: strong in mentoring relationships, open-minded.

Story 3:

Later in my career I joined a consulting company. Three months into my employment I was asked to participate in a "company cabaret." I've always been good at imitating politicians so I did my typical routine. Everyone thought it was very funny and my former colleagues still talk about it.

- My underlying skills: public speaking, charisma, visibility, humor.
- My values: public visibility, risk-taking, humor.
- Right work environment: creative, risk-taking.

Story 4:

I love to cook but usually only get to cook a gourmet meal once or twice a year. Then I decided I would have a millennium party featuring a gourmet dinner for 20. I thought about every detail. What would please each guest? What would bring them together? How to arrange the table? How to match each course with a particular wine? It was a great success. People still talk about the event and say it was one of the best gourmet dinners they ever had.

- My underlying skills: project management, organization, creativity, visibility, client orientation.
- My values: create lasting impact, family, trusted friends, cultural roots.
- Right working environment: strong sense of belonging, warmth.

Lauren then plotted each story against a list of leadership, management and selling skills (the table at the end of this chapter.). Then she ranked her skills according to the number of times they appeared in each story.

The skills that appeared in 4 stories or more were:

- Self management: taking initiative, personal risk taking and optimism.

- Social awareness: recognizing other constituencies' needs (clients, and sub-contractors).
- Leadership: source of inspiration for others, credibility with peers and management.
- Execution: ability to deliver on company vision.
- Managerial skills: problem solving, planning, project management.

After reviewing her key strengths, skills and values (and also after she completed the other assessments described below) Lauren identified four possible jobs:

- Associate Partner in a large consulting firm.
- Partner in a niche consulting firm.
- Director of Corporate Strategy or Corporate Development in a large manufacturing company.
- VP Strategy in a small manufacturing company.

She screened each job against her criteria and decided to contact 10 successful small specialized consulting companies in her geographic target area. She received three offers. She accepted one and is now a full Partner.

Don't forget to review past assessments

The value of past assessments is they will remind you of important themes. Anything that only appears once should be of little concern.

"This is Dr. Fredericks, the company's psychiatrist. He's here to determine whether or not you're disgruntled."

Past assessments to consider:

- **Any 360° feedback** you have received in the last few years. The power of a 360° is that you are hearing from the people who determine your success, your peers and your subordinates. While the boss's view is certainly important, experience has shown our real success is built based upon the relationship and perceptions of our peers and subordinates.
- **Past Performance Appraisals**. Well-written, balanced appraisals can contain real gold. Pay attention to what previous bosses have said about your strengths as well as your developmental challenges.
- **Peer Assessment** from leadership training programs. You have probably attended a number of leadership training programs over the past few years. Check to see how many had a feedback component. This will be particularly valuable if it was an outside program where the participants carried no political agenda and no historical baggage.
- **Self Assessment**. Pull out old self-assessments and see how they match your Seven Stories and your current assessment.

Fifteen-Year Vision

There was a terrific article in the *Harvard Business Review* (September–October, 1996) called "Building Your Company Vision" by James Collins and Jerry Porras. What struck us about the article was the power of their questions and how well they apply to a career plan. So we modified a few of them for you to consider as you do your Fifteen-Year Vision.

- What are my core values?
- What are my guiding principles?
- What are my 10-to-30-year "Big Hairy Audacious Goals (BHAG)?"

The first step in developing your Fifteen-Year Vision is to look at where you are today and then where you want to be in 5, 10 and 15 years. Yes the future is hard to predict but just say to yourself, "If I could control the future, how would I like my life to look?" Now go for it!

The Process

- First answer these questions for the present. It will give you a good base line.
- Then move to five years from now, answering the same questions.

- Do the same for 10 and 15 years, using the same questions.

The Questions

➤ What is your life like?

➤ Who is in your family, how old are they, what do they do?

➤ What is your relationship with your family members?

➤ Who are your friends? What do they do?

➤ Where are you living? What does it look like?

➤ How do you take care of your spiritual needs?

➤ How is your health? What do you do for exercise?

➤ What do you do for fun? What are your hobbies?

➤ How do you contribute to your community?

➤ What are your professional responsibilities?

➤ What else would you like to note about your life right now?

➤ Think about potential second or third careers.

➤ Are you doing any retirement planning? (Sooner is better these days!)

Identify Your Core Values

Your core values are your compass to assess the culture of the companies you will investigate. "Value clashes" are one of the most frequent reasons our clients decide to leave a company. It is critical to understand the values of potential peers and key leaders. As one client said, "if you work for a company that supports your values, you will thrive." We couldn't agree more.

How do you identify your values? Here are some techniques that will help:

1. Analyze your Seven Stories the way Lauren did.

2. If you owned a company, what core values would you like your company to embody?

3. Think of some of the leaders you have worked with or for and admired. What were their core values?

4. On the flip side: think of some of the "value clashes" you have had.

5. Check the mission statements of companies and charitable organizations you admire.

6. Talk about these values with family and friends.

Your Past

It is important to understand the past so history **does or doesn't** repeat itself. This is the classic "lessons learned" exercise.

We want you to quickly review the jobs you found exciting, rewarding and challenging. Think about your best two or three bosses and why were they the best? Remember those who were not and why. Armed with this information you will make much better career decisions going forward.

Satisfiers and Dissatisfiers

1. Make a list of the bosses, peers and board members with whom you worked in the last few jobs.

2. Make three columns. The first column will be those with whom you had **no serious problems**, the second column will be those with whom you had **some problems** and the last column are those with whom you had **serious problems**.

3. For the first column, ask yourself **why** you never had any serious problems? This step can lead to real insights.

4. Then look at the next two columns where there were challenges: What were the patterns? Consider the following:
   ✓ Was it a clash of styles?
   ✓ Was it a clash of values?
   ✓ Was it an ethical issue?
   ✓ Were there issues you could have avoided?
   ✓ If you could turn back the clock, is there anything you would do differently?

Putting Balance In Your Career Plan

It's very easy to slip into a life that gets out of balance where work takes over and your health, personal life and spiritual life take hits. So use your career transition to step back and look at what you want to achieve, not just in business but in your personal life.

The former CEO of Pepsi, Steve Reinemund, described his model for working towards balanced life:

"My success model is like a chair with four legs, the center (seat) is God. My family, friends, community and work are the four legs."

Some of our clients start the process of finding the "right job" by defining what the right life will look like. They pay attention to all aspects of their lives including family, health, fitness, fun, and spiritual needs not just the job.

How Do You Use Your Self-Assessment?

Here is some feedback from a few Five O'Clock Club clients about how they used their self-assessment.

Identify and demonstrate your strengths

"I leveraged my Seven Stories to improve the quality and texture of my accomplishments in the résumé, and cover letter."

"I kept reviewing my strengths before every interview as well as before writing my cover and follow-up letters and, believe it or not, before salary negotiation."

"I use to re-read my strengths on the days I was down."

Know your weaknesses because, sooner rather than later, someone will ask!

"Having made a list of my weaker areas, I carefully prepared for all those questions I hoped they wouldn't ask."

Know your core values. The odds of surviving a culture or boss that don't share your values are, in a word, lousy

"I was fortunate and had three offers to consider. I chose the one that was the closest to my value system even though it ended up being 15% below my other offers."

Remember the environments where you thrived and those you didn't

"I knew I couldn't survive another micro-manager. I needed a company that was strong on accountability and believed in giving the senior managers considerable leeway. Even though I knew this new position would stretch my leadership skills I accepted it, based upon my criteria."

"On paper, this was my best offer but after some in-depth discussions with the Director of IT, I realized we had very different management styles, as well as a different view about the company's IT strategy. It was the best offer I have ever turned down!"

Careful assessments are vital for determining your strengths, weaknesses, and goals in life in order to make the best choices, especially during a transition. You want to land and succeed in a great job but enjoy life too.

Define your possible jobs

Let's go back to Lauren's story. How did she actually select niche consulting companies as her primary target? Remember that at the end of her assessment, Lauren had a list of criteria that will be important to her in her new job.

As you can see, the Partner, Niche Consulting Firm and the VP of Strategy, small manufacturing company have the most "++". Using her Fifteen-Year Vision and brainstorming with her Advisory Board, Lauren decided to focus on the Niche Consulting Firm target first. (Targeting is covered in detail in Chapter 4).

Lauren's Criteria	Associate Partner Large Consulting Firm	Partner, Niche Consulting Firm	Director of Corporate Strategy or Corporate Dev. in large manufacturing company	VP of Strategy or Development in small manufacturing company
Her skills:				
entrepreneurship	+	++	–	++
creativity	–	+	+	+
autonomy	– –	++	– –	–
client orientation	+	++	+	++
analytics	++	++	++	+
team management	+	++	–	+
Her core values:				
independence	–	++	–	+
risk taking	–	++	+	++
recognition	+	++	+	++
The right working environment:				
small, close team	–	++	–	++
max. of 3 days of travel per week	–	–	++	+
Her long-term career vision				
General Manager of a mid-size, independent company	–	+	++	++

Chapter Summary ....

- Use The Five O'Clock Club assessment tools to get an accurate snapshot of your abilities and where you want to go.
- Include others in your quest. Ask for feedback from your former bosses, colleagues, best friends, and your significant other.
- Develop a specific roadmap. This process is all about **what is best for you** based on your strengths, your values, the environments where you have not only performed the best but had the most fun.

4
...

Targeting:
The Start Of An
Organized Search

Chapter Overview ....

- Defining your job targets around three dimensions: industry, position and geography
- Doing effective "market research" on your targets
- Avoiding speed bumps in the targeting phase

....

Quick Review

- You have just completed your Seven Stories and your Fifteen-Year Vision.
- You have a list of possible jobs in mind that matches your criteria.
- Now it is time to develop your **job targets**.

What is a Job Target?

Everything starts with your job targets. In fact, at the Five O'Clock Club we say "if your targets are wrong, everything is wrong." Your job targets are just like a sales rep's prospect list. And just as in sales, **nothing is going to close** if your job targets (prospects) are vague or ill-defined.

A job target contains three elements. Focusing on these three elements will allow you to logically begin to build the foundation for your job search.

1. **An industry** such as financial services, healthcare or data security **or company size**. Size is usually by revenue but could be, ROI, ROE, the number of employees or a combination.

2. A **specific position** (CFO, CTO, CMO, Controller, VP Human Resources, VP Finance) **or functional area** like finance, IT, or marketing.

3. **Geographic area** including international locations.

Target Companies

Your target companies are simply those where you can find your targeted jobs.

A job target is not necessarily an open position. It may be filled or it may not even exist . . . yet.

Our friend Lauren in Chapter 3 is a good example. One of the positions she targeted was at the Partner level with a U.S. consulting firm that did not have an office in France. However she discovered, during her networking, their strategy was to expand into Western Europe. She developed a plan for successful entry into this market and that's how she got an offer.

Another example in Lauren's search was a U.K. consulting firm that had no official openings at the Partner level. Lauren and one of the partners had a common friend and so it was easy for her to introduce herself. As the discussions progressed, they really wanted Lauren to join them and were ready to create a Partner position.

How Many Targets?

Just like a sales rep needs a strong prospect pipeline, you need a strong job target list. What is our definition of strong? At least 200. Five O'Clock Club research, over the last 25 years, has shown those clients who target at least 200 positions are usually the ones that land jobs the quickest.

Preliminary Target Investigation

What you would call a market probe, for a potential new product, we call a Preliminary Target Investigation. In this case the product is you. So your personal market probe is to find out whether "you" are going to sell into your targets.

Taking your time with Preliminary Target Investigation will help you avoid targeting opportunities that are unrealistic.

You may find out that one of your target companies has turned over three CFO's in 4 years, or the division you targeted is being spun off. You also may hear things like, "John, you just don't have quite the right skill sets," or "not enough industry experience" or "companies in this area hire 90% from the local market."

On the personal front, your spouse or significant other may tell you "I am not moving to Buffalo no matter what they pay you!"

So what will your Preliminary Target Investigation look like and how should you do it? Our suggested next steps are:

1. Develop a spread sheet, either electronic or paper, using the elements of a Job Target as your headings. (See Mark's case study below.)

2. Brainstorm all the possibilities under each heading. You can do this alone or with a trusted friend, mentor or colleague.

3. You now have a solid foundation for finding the specific companies that fall into each category: industries, size of company, specific positions and your geographic preferences.

4. Become your own research assistant and hit the web, the library and your network to find out the names of the companies fitting your criteria. And it could be a big number. However, bigger is better at this point.

5. Ways to begin to make your target list manageable and to focus your priorities:
   - ✓ Talk to peers, ex-bosses, and industry leaders about whether your list makes sense based upon your experiences and skill sets.
   - ✓ Apply performance criteria like ROE, revenue growth, rank in the market place, ala Jack Welch who said, "if we can't be #1 or #2 I don't want to be in the business."
   - ✓ Create an A, B and C list. Your A list would include the companies you would love to work for. Your B list are those that would be *OK* and your C List are

those you would not work for but where you can practice, test your market value and use their interest in you to leverage companies on your A and B list.

✓ If your A list is sizeable, rank your targets and work your way down the list. For example, if market place performance is most important then rank the A list accordingly.

6. Some of our clients also target "situations." So we suggest asking yourself questions like:

✓ Should I be looking at a "turnaround" situation?
   ✦ Sales turnaround?
   ✦ Profit turnaround?
   ✦ Customer service turnaround?
✓ Emerging market(s)?
✓ Running a family business?
✓ Not running a family business?

Research

This is the "market research" step of your search. We know you would never authorize a significant investment in a potential new product without thoroughly understanding and analyzing the potential markets and customers for the product. It is exactly the same for your job search.

So where do you find your target companies and good data about targets? There are three main sources: libraries, the Internet and networking.

The Library

• Make the research librarian your new best friend. They know where all the gold is buried.

They can point you to online resources as well as print resources. We know print may sound a bit old fashion but there are hundreds of great reference books out there that will give you additional targets, insights on your targets and point you in areas that will keep you on top of your game. (See the large appendix in our book *Shortcut Your Job Search: The Best Ways to Get Meetings*.) Here are three print examples from Gale Publications that contain a wealth of good information:

1. Encyclopedia of Associations: **Info on 20,000 Associations**.
2. Newsletters in Print: **10,000 Newsletters**.
3. Directories in Print: **Over 15,000 entries**.

✦ Check out public, community college, and university libraries. They frequently have access to different data bases.

TIPS:

✦ Don't drive around! Call first and ask for the research librarian.

✦ Ask if they have data bases that give you access to public companies, private companies and the not-for-profit sector.

✦ Do they offer online access from home if you are a member? For example, the New York Public Library does.

✦ Some libraries have access to LexisNexis which allows you to search by a company or individual name to see what has been written about them in the press and in industry publications over the years. This information can be invaluable **prior to an interview or networking meeting.**

The Internet

There is good news and bad news about the internet. The good news: It is the world's largest candy store of information. The bad news: It is the world's largest candy store of information. Examples: there are over 30,000 job sites. One inquiry can lead to over a million hits. So how do you sift through tons of data and what is the appropriate use of the internet in your search and research?

Google it first! (Or any search engine you like.)

One of the great features of Google is you can talk to it like a friend. For example, just typing in simple phrases like, "emerging bio-tech companies in Boston area" or "trends in fiber optics" or "latest financials on Xerox" gives you a wealth of info at your finger tips for your target research, your next interview, or an upcoming networking meeting.

We were tempted to give you a list of great research sites but we resisted. In this global internet age there is a "new great" practically every week.

So here is what you do: **before you start your research,** use your favorite search engine to find the "latest and greatest" research sites. Just type in "what are the best corporate research sites?" or "the best ways to do research on the internet" or "the best ways to find a profile on an executive." This will bring up the most recent articles and/or sites dealing with your question. Remember someone is always writing an article on the "ten best."

The bottom line is the Internet can be a very effective research tool. It can get you off to an incredibly fast start but please don't ignore the good old libraries and that wonderful "research assistant" called the Research Librarian.

Other Internet TIPS:

- Easiest way to find any *company's home page* is to Google it.
- Easiest way to begin your geographic targeting is to Google it.

Sample queries:

✓ New bio-tech companies in San Francisco Bay area?
✓ Largest health care companies in Boston?
✓ Wireless start-up companies in Dallas-Ft. Worth area?

How Mark Approached the Preliminary Targeting Exercise

Mark, a Five O'Clock Club client, is the VP of Strategy for a major European retail company. To develop his targets, he first looked at **Industry, Company Size, Geography and Position** but he also added some additional criteria like commitment to Research and Development (R&D), five-year growth rates, and return on equity (ROE).

Below is the table Mark used to begin his Targeting process.

Job Target Criteria	Metrics
• Industry	• Leisure Products such as: Boating, Watches, Fashion Accessories, Motorbikes, Consumer Electronics, Publishing, Toys, Cosmetics
	• Leisure Services such as: Travel, Hotels, Restaurants, Performing Arts, Marina management
• Company Size	• 500 million to 1 billion Euros
• Last 5 years growth rate	• 80th percentile of sector
• Last 5 years investments in R&D as a percentage of revenues	• 80th percentile of sector
• Last 5 years ROE	• 80th percentile of sector
• CEO profile	• International experience, breadth of functional experience, occupies leadership positions in industry associations, and is highly visible.
• Tenure of the CEO	• More than 5 years
• Average tenure of C-suite executives	• More than 5 years
• Geographical Location	• Western Europe
• Position	• VP Marketing or VP of Business Development

Mark next identified companies and job titles matching his criteria. Here is how he did it:

- He checked out both public and private companies by revenue using the **Ward's Business Directory** at his local library.
- The other financial information was collected from **Yahoo! Finance** and **10k's** for public companies.
- He also found the executive tenure from the 10k's and from company websites.
- Once he had the executive's names, he Googled them to find additional information and profiles.
- He identified about 150 companies and 200 positions.
- He divided the positions into 4 titles:
  - ✦ VP of Marketing for leisure products in Western Europe
  - ✦ VP of Business Development for leisure products in Western Europe
  - ✦ VP of Marketing for leisure services in Western Europe
  - ✦ VP of Business Development for leisure services in Western Europe

Mark's Results

- Eight weeks into his search he got his first verbal offer.
- By week 15, he had received 5 written offers.

Using Your Network

Your network is another potential wealth of information on people and companies you are targeting. We cover this in detail in Chapter 6 including:

- Efficient and effective ways of asking people in your network about your targets without having to make a 100 phone calls.
- How to expand your network.
- How to Avoid being perceived as a pest.
- The importance of making direct contacts.

Remember, the odds are, your next job will come from networking or direct contact. In fact almost every survey over the last 20 years has shown 70% or more of senior level jobs were found through networking or direct contact.

Speed Bumps To Avoid In the Targeting Phase

1. Not **targeting enough positions**. Again, you need at least 200 to have a timely search. Like the world of business, this is a numbers game.

   Remember a company may contain multiple targets for you. For example, a Fortune 50 company may have two or three jobs at your level. These jobs can be in major divisions or in stand alone subsidiaries.

2. Number two, **targeting industries only instead of companies**. This is a major trap. Targeting major sectors like healthcare or financial services, which contain thousands of companies in each, is guaranteed to slow your search.

   Think about it this way, if someone were to ask you if you knew anything about the healthcare industry, where would you start? But if someone asks you if you know anything about Blue Cross-Blue Shield of NJ, your mind immediately focuses and you start thinking, who do I know at Blue Cross-Blue Shield of NJ?

   Our point is, until you have the names of specific companies your search can never be focused and most of your networking meetings will be unproductive.

3. **Not doing enough research** on your A list. You must understand their financials, their performance in the industry, their reputation, pending legal issues and their competition. You will not be perceived as being on top of your game if you walk into a networking meeting or an interview without good data.

4. **Relying too much on one source**. Some of our clients only talk to a **few** trusted people which will lead to only a **few** contacts. *Harvey MacKay says, "If everyone in your network is just like you, it is not a network, it is an anthill."* (From *Dig Your Well Before You Are Thirsty.*)

5. **Doing too much research**. This is analogous to spending too much time surfing the internet. A good question for each of your specific targets is, "do I have enough information to be articulate on key issues?"

Chapter Summary ....

If you take away just one thing from this chapter it would be that **targeting is ultimately a numbers game**. You need to target 200 specific positions to have a timely search. The targets will be a combination of specific companies and positions that meet your criteria.

. . . .

5
···

"Packaging" Yourself: *The Best Way To Market . . . You!*

"You have to learn the rules of the game. And then you have to play better than anyone else." —Albert Einstein

Chapter Overview ....

- Your product launch
- Your Two-Minute Pitch and your Elevator Speech.
- Your world class résumé
- Your Marketing Plan and why it is critical
- Your No Nonsense cover letters

··

Your Product Launch

By now we hope you have done some research on your targets, gotten some feedback from trusted peers and a few mentors. You are reasonably comfortable with your targets so now it is time to think Product Launch.

One of the most important elements of a good product launch is having a great pitch and that pitch is communicated through the sales force, advertising and great collaterals. It is exactly the same for your job campaign.

- In this case **the product is . . . you.**
- The sales force is . . . you and your active network.
- **Your pitch** is your "Elevator Speech" and your **"Two-Minute Pitch."**
- **Your collateral materials and advertising** are your **résumé**, your **cover letters** and your **marketing plan.**
- **Consider using a mail campaign.** It is often ignored or underutilized. In Chapter 7 we will cover targeted and direct mail campaigns.

"Someone important is bound to see my résumé now."

We believe these are the tools that, if done well and executed well, will keep you in front of 90% of your competition.

Why Should We Hire You?

There is an additional step we recommend you take before your finalize your résumé and Two-Minute Pitch; it is your preparation for answering the question that is on everyone's mind who interviews you. Why should we hire you? Some ask it directly but everyone is thinking it so why not prepare your answer well in advance? Not only will it improve the quality of your résumé and pitch but also the quality of your interviews.

We would like to share with you how one of our clients, Sophia, prepared for "why should we hire you?"

Background: Sophia is the International Director of Supply Chain for a pharmaceutical company responsible for North America and Western Europe. She has decided she would like to move into the alcoholic beverage industry.

Her process: First, she outlined everything she could think of that described the current supply chain challenges beverage companies were facing. A few examples from her notes:

- Full integration between sales, marketing, operations and logistics for increased supply chain flexibility at the lowest cost.
- Implementation of a Continuous Improvement/Six Sigma culture to improve delivery times and lower operating costs.
- Maximize global sourcing.

Next she outlined her skills and how they apply to the industry challenges. Some of her skills were:

- Expert in change management, Six Sigma and supply chain optimization.
- Developed and implemented a post-merger global supply optimization program in North America for a drinkable children's medication. Savings, $180 million across 140 global sites.
- Have led lead over a dozen multi-functional teams in multi-cultural environments.

Last, Sophia made sure she integrated all the relevant data into her résumé and Two-Minute Pitch.

This process allows you to make sure the language and results in your résumé and your pitch match what your targeted companies (or industry as in Sophia's case) are looking to hear and see.

TIP: This is also an excellent process to repeat **before every interview**.

Your *Two-Minute Pitch*

At the Five O'Clock Club we say, "if your pitch . . . the way you position yourself . . . is wrong, everything about your search is wrong." This is tough love but put yourself back in your company in the planning phase of a major product launch. Wouldn't you, the CEO or the SVP of Marketing be telling the troops "we can have a dynamite launch but if the positioning is wrong it won't matter!"

The *Two-Minute Pitch* is often the answer to, "So tell me about yourself."

TIP: Before answering the "tell me about yourself" question we suggest you ask the following:

1. Situation: If you do not know what the key challenges are. Your response to the "tell me about yourself" question is this: "Before we get started would you mind sharing the key challenges for this position?"
2. Situation: If you know the key challenges but you need to re-confirm, you can take the lead immediately by saying something like: "I understand your number one priority is opening a new plant in Brazil followed closely by taking costs out of the old plant, is that correct?"

In our experience these questions work at least 80% of the time, which means their answers will help you tailor your *Two-Minute Pitch*.

The key elements of a Two-Minute Pitch:

- First, understand your audience. To whom are you pitching?
- Next, keep in mind, what are they are looking for, **not** what you want them to know.

If they are looking for someone to turn around an organization, build a team or take costs out of the business then your pitch has to demonstrate **in a compelling way** how you meet those needs. Compelling means to communicate with a **good story** supported by **measurable results**.

- It allows the decision makers to see you as appropriate for the job.

Here are is an example of a *Two-Minute Pitch* from Janet:

Situation: The company you are interviewing with is about to open their first plant in Brazil. You are interviewing with the CEO.

In your last assignment you were a key member of the team that opened plants in Brazil and Mexico.

Janet's Pitch: John, I understand the challenge here is to be the point person for opening your company's first plant in Brazil by October 1 with at least 85% nationals. (Tip: Be sure to clarify this point with a simple, is that correct? You don't want the CEO correcting you half way through your pitch!)

At ABC, Inc. we were really under the gun because not only did we have to get Brazil on line but also Mexico and they were opening within two months of each other and my boss had no mercy (said with a smile). He wanted to open with 100% nationals! The good news is we opened both plants on time, within budget and with 95% nationals. The other good news is both plants exceeded their first six-month production goals by 12.5% and their retention goals by 37%.

Two-Minute Pitch Summary

Was Janet's pitch **compelling**? You bet! In a nice way she told the CEO she can beat his target and then some.

You can also see this wasn't literally a pitch that took two minutes. The reason we say *Two-Minutes* is you need to have a solid *Two-Minutes of* **compelling** data to share not just about the top priorities but also about what else you bring to the table.

CAUTION. Where some of our clients stumble in the interview:

They deliver a great pitch but they stumble answering some of the probes. Why? They thought they could wing it because it was a fairly recent experience. Many of the probes will be easy to answer but the little things will catch you up.

Using our "plant in Brazil" example, you would be prepared to answer the following questions; "How did you pull that off?" "**Who were your contacts** in the Brazilian government?" "How were you able to achieve a hiring rate of 95% nationals." "What were the elements of your retention strategy?"

If you were winging it the probe that could cause you to stumble would be remembering all the names and titles of your Brazilian contacts.

TIP: Write out the answers so the details are fresh. We recommend putting the answers on 3 × 5 cards because they allow you to review them most anywhere, including waiting to meet the CEO.

Elevator Speech

Unlike the *Two-Minute Pitch,* this is literally a pitch you could give someone while riding on the elevator, in a hall way, or at the gym. It is for those times when **you only have seconds**–not minutes–to make an impression. It is often the answer to the small-talk question, "what do you do?" or "what are you up to these days?"

Just like the *Two-Minute Pitch*, **it has to be compelling** and you have very little time to deliver it. So what might an elevator speech sound like?

Someone in the "elevator" has just asked you, "so Mary, what are you up to these days?" Mary's answer: "I am a product manager with XYZ and am really pumped. We just wrapped up a terrific launch that exceeded all its market share goals." (This is 25 words and can be delivered in 10 seconds.) **Compelling**? We think so. Mary was able to say she was on a winning team with just the facts, no hyperbole.

This sounds easy but it is not. Most of us take the easy way out, knowing we don't have much time, and say, "oh, I am still a product manager with XYZ." Unfortunately that response means you lost a golden opportunity for more dialogue about your team's accomplishments and the role you played. Why? The compelling Elevator Speech often gets a follow-up statement like, "Mary, that's great. I would like to hear more about it. Let's set up a time to chat."

TIP: **Assume this will happen to you** and have some punchy compelling responses prepared and keep them updated with your latest accomplishments. We have two clients, in the last year, who literally landed great jobs by being prepared with their Elevator Speech. However we have to admit both happened at local fitness centers not in elevators.

Would You Like to Have a World-Class Résumé?

We are going to share with you the elements of a world class résumé, but before we do that let's clear up a few popular **résumé myths**.

"Résumés are like religion and politics, everyone has an opinion."

- Résumé Myth #1. Your résumé should be just one page and definitely never more than two pages. How many times have you heard that?

Truth: Your résumé can be almost any length **as long as the content is compelling**. What does that mean? If your résumé contains hard-hitting results then people will turn the pages. True accomplishments make for compelling reading whether it is your résumé, a favorite sports figure's stats, or the profile of a political or religious leader.

- Résumé Myth #2. Always tell them your job objective.

Truth: Twenty years ago this was the conventional wisdom. Today a specific job objective is much too limiting. Contemporary résumés start with a positioning statement which succinctly tells the reader several critical things; your level, your functional expertise, and your industry (or industries) expertise.

TIP: Always tailor the positioning statement to whomever you are pitching. Here is one example from the top of an actual résumé:

Senior Global Marketing Executive
*with over 20 years experience successfully launching consumer products
and penetrating new markets in North America, South America and the Far East.*

In 26 words you have communicated that you are a highly experienced global executive who understands that marketing is all about growing the business.

- Résumé Myth #3. Be sure to include all your responsibilies.

Truth: Again, this was the conventional wisdom twenty years ago and for good reason. In the "old days" jobs were evaluated heavily based upon responsibilities. Today it's all about the results. So what should you say about your responsibilities? Just the most critical: P&L, revenue, operating budget, functions managed and number of professionals you are responsible for. This should be covered in two lines under each of your job titles.

- Résumé Myth #4. Be sure to tell them something personal.

Truth: Personal information is a two-edged sword. If you mention things like golf, sailing, or flying half the readers will resonate with your interests. However, half will not. Our advice is to leave it off . . . unless you know the decision maker loves golf! In fact some of our clients have discovered this by Googling the executive.

What is the most important part of your résumé?

The **summary section is the most important part of your résumé.** It is the first few inches of your résumé. Because it is read first, it is truly the "first impression." In effect, the summary section becomes an "executive summary" of your entire résumé. Here is one example and we will explain each section below.

ROBERT S. WOOD

244 Elmwood Drive   C (717) 899-8888
York, PA 17404   rsw@anywhere.com   O (717) 727-3339

(First, is your Positioning Statement)

SENIOR OPERATIONS EXECUTIVE
with a unique blend of financial and operational experience including supply chain, information systems, human resources, facilities and procurement.

Expertise

(Expertise: you were one of the key "go to" people in each of the areas you mention or the resident expert.)

- Private Equity Turnaround
- Strategic Planning & Execution
- Corporate & Business Unit Leadership
- Human Resources Strategist

- Mergers, Acquisitions & Divestitures
- Financial Reporting & Controls
- Treasury Management
- Business Process Reengineering

Results

(Results: should include five or six of your best results from your last two to three jobs.)

➤ Provided key operational and financial leadership for a private equity turnaround, which improved EBITDA by more than 200% in two years.

➤ Led the acquisition and financing of a $180 million European manufacturing company.

➤ Spearheaded development of a pricing model resulting in revenue growth of 18%.

➤ Created a highly profitable eBusiness. Achieved breakeven within 3 months.

➤ Sponsored employee development programs aimed at increasing throughput; operational performance improved by more than 15%.

➤ Secured five $150+ million public and private debt offerings.

Recognized For

(Recognized For: This is what your bosses have said about you. TIP: Check your formal appraisals in the last few years. They will have some good descriptors of your performance and leadership qualities.)

• Superior Executer • Financial Integrity • Leadership • Effective Team Builder
• Superb Communicator • Champion for Leadership Development

Summary Section Explanation

You have just read Robert's summary. This is just one format you may choose to use. There are several more examples in Table 1. However there are a few areas, we feel, you **must** include.

The **first must** is the **Positioning Statement**.

> It has two parts. One establishes your level and either your functional or operational expertise. EGS: Global CFO, International Marketing Executive, Corporate CTO, COO Latin American Division. You do not have to use your current title.
>
> The second part of your positioning statement is the "gold." It should separate you from the pack. It is what makes you unique.

Senior Global Marketing Executive

with over 20 years' experience successfully launching consumer products and penetrating new markets in North America, South America and the Far East.

> In this example, the combination of 20 years' experience in consumer products, and penetrating new markets in North America, South America and the Far East, is what separates this marketing executive from other global marketing executives.

The **second must** are your **Results**.

Results immediately answer the question on every decision makers mind, "what can you do for us?" Let's stay with our Global Marketing Executive example. Here is a result that could be in the Summary Section:

✦ Launched four skin care products in Brazil that reached number one or two in their category within six months and **all exceeded their revenue targets by more than 20%.**

The **third must** is your **Expertise**.

Experienced managers and executives have accumulated, by definition, lots of expertise so make sure you capture it in your summary. Remember you don't have to be the "published expert," but you do need to be considered one of the key "go to people" in each area you list.

Clients ask us how many areas should they list? Our rule of thumb is 6 to 8.

Other areas you should consider including:

• Industry or company experience. Mentioning several industries, just under your positioning statement, shows breadth and sets up the discussion of why you will be successful in a new industry. Also if you have worked for some "household names" be certain to list them. This is how it would look using company names:

Senior Global Marketing Executive

With over 20 years' experience successfully launching consumer products and penetrating new markets in North America, South America and the Far East.

Procter and Gamble   **Gillette**   **Colgate-Palmolive**

- Languages you are fluent in as well as any unique or prestigious degree you may have. These can go at the end of the summary section or under the Positioning Statement.
- The **Recognized For** section is to capture what your bosses and other references will say about you. It can't be what you think they will say. It truly has to be what they have said.

    It frequently prompts the interviewer to ask, "what is this *recognized for* section all about?" Your answer, "it is a combination of things highlighted in my performance reviews and what several of my recent managers have told me personally."

Summary of the Summary Section

- **Most important TIP.** Your positioning statement, results and expertise should always be tailored to your audience, i.e., your targeted companies or industries.
- Everything you decide to put into the Summary Section also stays in its normal place in the résumé. So a key result is in two places, under the Summary Section and under the company where the result took place.
- **Bolding and <u>underlining</u>**. We all understand the importance of using bolding and underlining to catch the readers eye in a good print advertisement but many of us are reluctant to use this technique in our résumé. We **<u>strongly suggest</u>** you use the technique. It literally forces the eye to focus on your accomplishments because the eye can not skip over a bolded and underlined word.
- There are three examples of Summary Sections at the end of this chapter on pages 59-60.

What Goes Into the Body of the Résumé?

Below is the basic template, covering just one position.

FYPON, LTD.,	York , Pennsylvania	2002–2005

*Leading US manufacturer of polyurethane flooring. Revenue $36M. Customers include dominant one and two step channel partners of building products, including **Home Depot**.*

Executive Vice President & Chief Financial Officer
*Responsible for all financials, business unit operations, procurement, human resources and information systems. Staff: 18. Budget: $2.5M. **Board Member and Equity Partner**.*

- Provided operational and financial leadership for the turnaround of this private equity company. <u>**EBITDA increased by more than 200%**</u> within two years.
  - ➤ These results positioned the company for exit, as the <u>**market value for the company grew exponentially**</u> over this two year period.

- Led team to develop an automated custom pricing system to assure profitable custom segment growth. Metrics were established to focus on accountability and measure success.
  - ➤ <u>**Sales volume grew by more than 18%**</u> for the custom business segment.

- Significantly enhanced the company's financial controls and processes to dramatically improve the continuity of financial reporting.
  - ➤ <u>**Aged AR reduced by 90% and reserve for obsolete inventory reduced 75%**</u>.

The format for the body of the résumé hasn't changed in years. The key points are:

- Your experience is listed in reverse chronological order which means your current or last job is listed on the first page.
- The first line is always the company name, the location, and your total years of service.
- The next line is a brief, meaning no more than two lines, description of the company, its products, revenue and, if appropriate, key customers.
- Next is the title of the last job you held with the company. If you had several

jobs within the company, list each job separately with the title and the tenure for that job.

- For each job, list your key responsibilities in no more than three lines.
- Last, your bulleted results for each job. Bullets work well because they are much easier for the eye to scan.

TIP: A paragraph format is dated and more difficult to read. We suggest not writing in narrative form.

- A good results bullet is quantifiable. The ideal quantification is "with the numbers" but that isn't always possible. If you can't quantify with numbers then look for qualitative measures. A qualitative example would be, "the CEO said it was the best financial Board presentation she had ever seen."
- Questions you should ask yourself as you write your accomplishments:
  - ✦ Did it improve the top line?
  - ✦ Did it improve the bottom line?
  - ✦ Did it lower costs?
  - ✦ Did it improve the internal or external customer's experience?
  - ✦ Did it help acquire or retain customers?

These are the fundamental drivers of any business.

Please see pages 61-70 for several résumé examples.

Your Marketing Plan: Never Leave Home Without It!

Why Do You Need a Marketing Plan and What Is It?

- A Marketing Plan is simply a one-page document to be used in networking meetings.
- It allows your networking contacts to laser focus on your targeted companies. As they scan your list of target companies they cannot help thinking, "who do I know at Merck, or IBM or CitiGroup?"
- It allows you to focus the discussion on your most important targets.
- It shows people you are focused and organized.

What Does It Look Like?

Marketing plan for Donna Smith:

Donna Smith

314 S. Scotch Avenue

Wilton, NJ 07777

(888) 518-8888

dsmith@comcast.net

Senior Marketing Manager

*with a track record of successful new product launches and re-launches
that consistently captured market share.*

Expertise

- *Commercial development of pipeline products*
- *Optimizing the product portfolio*

- *Product life cycle management*
- *Cross functional team leadership*

Industry Experience

Wyeth	*VP, Healthcare Marketing*	2001–2006
Genentech	*Director Healthcare Marketing*	1996–2001
McNeil Pharmaceutical	*Senior Market Research Analyst*	1990–1996
GlaxoSmithKline	*Marketing/Financial Analyst*	1986–1990

Key Results

- **Established division profitability** ahead of forecast by re-launching a key HIV product.
- Focused product positioning and marketing launch plans for several oncology products leading to **increasing sales 45% over 3 years to $100M.**
- Created and implemented post-merger marketing strategy for $100M hospital business by capitalizing on major changes in healthcare reimbursement **driving company's market share from fifth to first.**

Education

George Washington University BA   Wharton MBA

Pharma Targets

- Berlex Laboratories
- Bristol-Myers Squibb
- Hoffman-La Roche Inc

- Merck & Co, Inc
- Novartis Pharmaceutical Corp
- Organon Inc

- Pfizer Inc
- Sanofi-Aventis
- Schering-Plough Corp

Specialty and Biotech Targets

- Biovail Corp
- Celgene Corp
- Cytogen Corp
- Dov Pharmaceutical Inc.

- Eisai Inc.
- Forest Labs Inc.
- Genta Inc.
- Imclone Systems, Inc.

- Ortho Biotech Inc
- Reliant Pharmaceutical
- Sankyo Pharm Inc
- The Medicines Company

Industry Leaders and Experts

(List a few leaders and experts in your targeted industry you would like to meet.)

The Basic Format of Your Marketing Plan

- It is similar to a one-page résumé; it is very condensed.
- The **positioning statement** should be a direct lift from your résumé.
- The **expertise** section should include your top 4–6 areas.
- **Experience** is just the company name, your last title and your total tenure.
- **Key results** should be your top 3–5 "home runs." Be sure to include significant awards or key recognition you have received: "recognized by the CEO for having the most profitable division in the company last year."
- **Education.** Just the school(s) and degree.
- **Your "A" targets.** The rest of your Marketing Plan should list the companies you would most like to work for as well as key industry executives or industry experts you would like to meet.
- If you have more "A" targets than can fit on one page, good for you! Please use a second page to include those as well as your "B" and "C" targets. However, we suggest that if you have a two-page Marketing Plan, bring the extra page with you. For your emails and initial discussions start with just the first page. You don't want to overwhelm them.

What Are the Best Ways To Use Your Marketing Plan?

- Take it to every networking meeting, including group meetings.
- We recommend emailing your Marketing Plan rather than your résumé before a networking meeting. Sending your résumé communicates you want to talk about job openings and you don't. You are just looking for good data on your targets and your Marketing Plan reinforces this. However always take several copies of your résumé with you in case they ask for it or you get lucky and there happens to be an appropriate opening.
- Develop a set of questions appropriate to your target companies and your expertise. Some suggested questions to ask at a networking meeting are:
  - ✦ I am looking to learn more about Merck's marketing approaches in the "xyz area."
  - ✦ I understand ABC, Inc. just hired a new CEO and he is really shaking things up. Have you heard anything about that?
  - ✦ In 2004 Eisai Medical Research opened new headquarters in Ridgefield Park, NJ. Are you familiar with the company?

  These are very specific questions. The specificity demonstrates you are serious, and not just fishing for names. Few of your competitors will go to this trouble so you will immediately set yourself apart.

Cover Letters

Nearly everyone feels challenged in this area so you are not alone if you do too! We are going to give you the important fundamentals for each type of letter based on the successes Five O'Clock Club clients have had over the past 25 years.

There are four basic cover letters you will be dealing with in your campaign:

1. Your letter to retained search firms (in this chapter)
2. Your response to an ad (in this chapter)
3. Your targeted mail campaign (chapter 7)
4. Your direct mail campaign (chapter 7)

Cover Letters to Retained Search Firms

As part of your campaign strategy you need to write to "retained search firms." As you know these are the search firms companies contract with to find managers and professionals at the $150k and above level. They are distinguished from "contingency search firms" by the fact they get paid even if the job isn't filled . . . providing they have presented a set number of qualified candidates. Contingency firms do not get paid unless someone is hired.

We are focusing on retained firms. However if you have a great contact at a contingency firm you should definitely use it. If you choose to write some contingency firms be sure to tell them you do not want your résumé distributed without your express permission.

There are basically three circumstances where you will be contacting retained search firms:

1. One of your peers, mentors or bosses has suggested you write a specific person at a specific firm and they have given you permission to use their name.

2. Your network has tipped you off that a search firm is working on a search appropriate for your experience, level and skill sets but you have no one's name you can use.

3. You conduct a direct mailing to all the retained search firms specializing in your target markets.

The best single resource for these mailings is, *The Directory of Executive Recruiters* by Kennedy Information, often referred to as the "Red Book." They have been publishing this directory for over 30 years.

A FEW TIPS:

- This directory is annual so it is reasonably current. It contains the contact information including the names of the recruiters for nearly every office in the world. However we recommend calling each office you are contacting to verify the information is current, or at least check their website.
- If it is not clear who runs the practice covering your target area(s), ask the receptionist, "would you mind sharing with me who is currently heading up the healthcare sector?"

Once you have identified the recruiters in your target markets, you are ready to write the cover letter. The format is very basic. They are not interested in any kind of pitch: each office gets literally hundreds of résumés a day. Their first sorting is to see if your functional expertise and comp level fit a current search they are working on. They do not carefully scrub your résumé at this point. Here is what they want to see in the cover letter:

- Your title and company name.
- **Briefly**, your area of expertise.

Include support of your expertise. For example if you are a VP of Sales you would include two or three, not a laundry list, of some significant quantifiable results. Use a bullet format. It might look like this:

- In my last three assignments we have exceeded all sales and customer retention targets by at least 15%.
- Last year we landed the largest major account in the company's history worth over $40M in annual revenue.
- Your current total compensation package.
    + This is the **only situation** where you volunteer compensation information.
    + Depending on your situation this can be expressed in terms of your last full year compensation package (base plus bonus) or an average of the last several years, whichever is greater.
- They also want to know if you will relocate.
- Always attach your résumé.

The only difference in each of your cover letters is your opening line.

- Referral: Dear Bob, Mary Altman the CFO at Borden Instruments suggested I contact you. I am currently the SVP of Marketing at Zeon Instruments. **Short and to the point.**
- Tipped off about an opening: Bob, I understand you are currently working on a search for an SVP of Marketing for a high tech technical instruments company. I am currently the SVP of Marketing at Zeon Instruments and would be interested in learning more about the opportunity. **Bob can immediately see you are in the ball park: right industry, right level.**
- Direct mailing: Dear Bob, I am a senior marketing executive, most recently as the SVP of Marketing at Zeon Instruments and prior to that the VP Sales at ABC Instruments. **Stay away from detailed explanations of why you are no longer there unless it is real clean i.e. "we were just sold and the acquiring company has a very competent SVP of Marketing."**

There is an example of a retained search firm cover letter on page 73.

Cover Letter For an Ad or Job Posting

Most of you know the drill here. For those who haven't answered an ad or a job posting for some time remind yourself; what is the reader looking for? It is simply, do you meet their critical requirements or not?

So first list the requirements from the ad or posting, especially the "must haves." Then decide which of your measurable results, professional qualifications and responsibilities best demonstrate you meet their needs.

We suggest the following format:

- Opening paragraph refers to the ad or posting **using their exact wording.** For example: I am responding to your May 6 ad in the WSJ for the VP Business Development. Also add any reference numbers mentioned.
- Next list each requirement and how you meet it. You can format this vertically where you list the first requirement then how you meet it or horizontally, the old Ben Franklin technique, where you use two columns.

See pages 71 and 72 for an example of each.

Here is one example using the vertical format:

(Lifted directly from their ad)

"We are looking for a Director of Product Marketing who has experience launching multiple products every year."

(Your response)

"Over the last three years I have averaged 4 new product launches and 7 product enhancements across multiple market segments, including Europe and South America."

- Add anything that might be of significant value to them that they haven't asked for such as being multilingual, having a unique degree, or professional certification. This is also the place to share any unique knowledge you have of the company, industry or market place.
- Closing. Keep it simple, "I look forward to learning more about this opportunity."
- Good idea to attach your résumé.

Cover Letters for Direct and Targeted Mailings

In Chapter 7 we will discuss the importance of doing direct and targeted mailings as part of your search strategy. We will discuss the formats for these cover letters in that section. By the way, some studies show that over 20% of all jobs are found through direct-mail campaigns.

Chapter Summary ·······································

- **The Two-Minute Pitch.** It is not a canned pitch. It should be tailored to your audience. It **must contain** how you can get done what they need to get done.
- **Your Résumé.** Three critical areas that need to be on point: your positioning statement, your summary section and your quantifiable results. These all answer the question on every hiring manager's mind, "what can this candidate do for us?"
- **Your Marketing Plan.** Use it at every networking meeting.
- **Cover letters.** Don't be afraid to test market them. Ask several senior level retained search executives you know to comment on your cover letter to search firms. Do the same with your cover letter for an ad or posting. Ask someone you know in HR or a respected hiring manager what they think of your letter.

Table 1. Three Examples of the Summary Section of the résumé

Mary V. Allison

Senior Executive

with 20 years of CFO, CAO, Corporate Counsel and general management experience.

Expertise

• IPO's • Raising venture capital • Mergers and Acquisitions
• Start-ups • Turn arounds • Financial Planning and Budgeting
• Sophisticated financial control systems • International

- Raised more than *$300 million in capital* through IPO's, VC's public and private means, public debt placements, Reg D private placements, securitization of receivables, and commercial bank loans;
- Negotiated and closed *mergers and acquisitions* with a market value *of over $275 million* in *domestic and international* settings;
- Implemented over *a dozen financial control systems* including *SAP, Peachtree, and Real World*;
- Developed and executed business plans *growing company from annual revenues of $8 million to $100 million in two years*;
- Actively participated in corporate governance for client as *member of board of directors*.

MBA   CPA   JD

. . . .

Randy Clapp

Senior IT Executive

20 years of domestic and international experience with a reputation for delivering value and lowering costs.

Reduced IT spending by $10M
Tripled revenues while decreasing costs by 30%
Implemented a process across peer groups that increased profitability by $25M

Industries:	Big 5 Consulting • Travel and Hospitality • Managed Care • Financial • Manufacturing
Expertise:	growing revenue • taking costs out of the business • targeted outsourcing • business relationships • project management (PMI, SEI-CMM) • cross functional team leadership
Recognized for:	leadership • change agent • delivering results • sense of urgency

. . . .

William C. Baines

Vice President of Sales

25+ years of experience, managing direct and channel sales organizations, within both domestic and international markets.

Business Results

- Achieved 53% revenue and 38% margin growth at Acadia.
- Created first muti-million dollar channel organization for the US at Malitor International.
- Contributed $11M of Malitor's revenue through distribution partnerships.
- Generated $12.6M in sales at Actel Link Communications.
- Consistently in the top 10% of revenue and margin producers.

Professional Experience

- Strong management skills, including the development of strategic sales teams.
- Major Account experience with G.E, Coca-Cola, Goldman-Sachs, Apple Computer, Time-Warner, and Bank of America.
- Significant International experience in Latin America, Asia-Pacific, and Europe.
- Proficient with the use and management of sales force automation applications including Siebel, ONYX, ACT, and Goldmine.

Industry Expertise

- Telecommunications: Network, applications, and infrastructure.
- Call Center applications: Focus on Banking and Financial Services including software development and web services.

Table 2 Complete Résumés

ROBERT S. WOOD

244 Elmwood Drive   C (717) 899-8888
York, PA 17404   rsw@anywhere.com   O (717) 727-3339

SENIOR EXECUTIVE

with a unique blend of financial and operational experience including supply chain, information systems, human resources, facilities and procurement.

Expertise

- Private Equity Turnaround
- Strategic Planning & Execution
- Corporate & Business Unit Leadership
- Human Resources Strategist

- Mergers, Acquisitions & Divestitures
- Financial Reporting & Controls
- Treasury Management
- Business Process Reengineering

Results

- Provided key operational and financial leadership for a private equity turnaround, which **improved EBITDA by more than 200%** in two years.
- **Led the acquisition** and financing of a $180 million European manufacturing company.
- **Led the divestiture** of a $170 million distressed business.
- Spearheaded development of a pricing model resulting in **revenue growth of 18%**.
- **Created a highly profitable eBusiness.** Achieved breakeven within 3 months.
- Sponsored employee development programs aimed at increasing throughput; **operational performance improved by more than 15%**.
- **Secured five $150+ million public and private debt offerings**.

Recognized For

• Superior Executer • Financial Integrity • Leadership • Effective Team Builder
• Superb Communicator • Champion for Leadership Development

FYPON, LTD., York, Pennsylvania   2002–2005
The leading US manufacturer of polyurethane millwork. Revenue $36 million. Customers include dominant one and two step channel partners of building products, including the Home Depot.

Executive Vice President & Chief Financial Officer

Responsible for all financials, business unit operations, procurement, human resources and information systems. Staff of 18, budget of $2.5 million. **Board Member and Equity Partner.**

ROBERT S. WOOD, Page Two

- Provided operational and financial leadership for the turnaround of this private equity company. EBITDA increased by more than 200% within two years.
  ➤ These results positioned the company for exit, as the **market value for the company grew exponentially over this two year period**.

- Facilitated the strategic plan to solidify the company's leading market position and to enable revenue growth through new initiatives to increase the market demand for molded millwork.
  ➤ **Sales volume grew approximately 10%** and operational metrics improved materially.
- Led team to develop an automated custom pricing system to assure profitable custom segment growth. Metrics established to focus on accountability and measure success.
  ➤ **Sales volume grew by more than 18%** for the custom business segment.
- Significantly enhanced the company's financial controls and processes to dramatically improve the continuity of financial reporting.
  ➤ **Aged AR reduced by 90% and reserve for obsolete inventory reduced by 75%.**
- Developed an e-business platform for the company's products, together with other products in the building products industry.
  ➤ The e-business model achieved breakeven within 3 months.
- Sponsored the establishment of mentoring, incentive and leadership development programs that improved throughput and reduced labor costs.
  ➤ **Operational performance improved 15%.**

GLATFELTER, York, Pennsylvania   1981–2002
A $725 million, 3,400 employee manufacturer of specialty papers and engineered products, with operations in the US, Europe and the Philippines. Customers included large publishers (R.R. Donnelly & Time Warner) and specialty products converters (3M & DuPont).

Chief Strategy Officer   2000–2002
Corporate responsibility for strategic planning and business development.
- Chaired a team to **develop a corporate Balanced Scorecard,** which enabled the company's strategy and related initiatives to be clearly measured and communicated.
  ➤ One resulting initiative was the creation of a new products development function, with related business processes, which increased specialty sales materially in subsequent years.
- Led corporate team in a $170 million divestiture of a Division which no longer fit the company's strategic profile. Also negotiated a 3-year $20 million supply agreement with new owners.

ROBERT S. WOOD, *Page Three*

Corporate Vice President Administration   1998–2000

Responsibility for supply chain, including procurement and transportation, public and governmental relations, corporate human resources, labor relations, environmental affairs and aviation. Staff: 60, budget: $6.5 million.

- Implemented a supply chain cost reduction program, which enhanced cash flow by $15 million.
- Developed and implemented a logistics solution for key manufacturing facility, including long-haul transportation, jockeying and warehouse services.
- Implemented reorganization programs to remain cost competitive in an oversupplied industry.
  - ➤ **Reduced annual costs of wages and benefits by $9 million**.
- Represented the company's interests in a **multi-billion dollar Superfund clean up** of the Fox River including developing tactics for legal defense and scientific research, and interfacing with federal and state regulators.
  - ➤ Negotiated a new allocation of interim group expenses for potentially responsible parties; Glatfelter's share was reduced materially, **saving millions of dollars**.
- Led negotiations with the DEP and EPA to secure a consent decree and wastewater treatment permit **with standards that were technically and economically feasible**.
- Led the company's **successful ISO 14001 certification process**.

Corporate Secretary & Treasurer   1992–1998

Responsible for all legal and financial affairs including all SEC filings. Staff of 9, budget of $2.5 million.

- Negotiated and closed company's debt financing transactions from 1992 to 1998, including public bonds, revolving credit facilities and industrial revenue bonds.
  - ➤ **Rates and spreads were very competitive** with comparably rated securities.
- Responsible for the company's **$450M+ pension portfolio**, managed through leading investment managers, including JP Morgan, Warburg Pincus and Ruane, Cunniff & Goldfarb.
  - ➤ Portfolio's performance **consistently outperformed the SEI balanced equity index**.
- Led a team that negotiated a $180M acquisition of a global European company.
  - ➤ The representations, warranties and indemnities negotiated with this deal **saved the company millions** due to the exposure of the acquired company to undefined legal claims.
- Completed a feasibility study for the purpose of establishing a **Chinese joint venture**.

ROBERT S. WOOD, *Page Four*

Assistant Secretary & Assistant Treasurer	1987–1992
Solutions Integrator and Microcomputer Manager	1985–1987
Financial Analyst	1981–1985

EDUCATION

MBA, Wharton, 1981

BS in Accounting, University of Pennsylvania, 1979

EXECUTIVE DEVELOPMENT

The CFO, The Strategic Partner to the CEO, Wharton Executive Business School

Management of Managers Program, University of Michigan Business School

RANDY CLAPP   21 Elm Rd Wilton, Ct 06612

rc@anywhere.net (203) 233 3333

Senior IT Executive

20 years of domestic and international experience
with reputation for delivering value and lowering cost.
Reduced IT spending by $10M
Tripled revenues while decreasing costs by 30%
Implemented a process across peer groups that increased profitability by $25M

Industries: • Big 5 Consulting • Travel and Hospitality • Managed Care • Financial
• Manufacturing

Expertise: • growing revenue • taking costs out of the business • targeted outsourcing
• business relationships • project management (PMI, SEI-CMM) • cross
functional team leadership

Recognized for: • leadership • change agent • delivering results • sense of urgency

---

CENDANT CORPORATION Parsippany, NJ   2001–present

Vice President of Technology for Avis Rent a Car
Reporting to the Chief Information Officer, lead a Strategic Management team responsible for major IT initiatives and customer relationships. Staff of 100+ IT professionals and budget of $40M Performed due diligence upon Cendant's acquisition of Avis that resulted in the reduction of $10M+ in annual IT spending.

- Redesigned an IT organization that placed focus on customer relationships, project management, and 3rd party leverage that drove predictability and compressed timelines into the organization.
- Turned around major technology initiatives including web development, data warehouse, imaging, and wireless systems through selective vendor partnering and offshore development.

OXFORD HEALTH PLANS Trumbull, CT   1999–2001

Director of Program Management for Information Systems
Reporting to the Chief Information Officer, served as internal consultant to Information Systems division 400+ technology professionals with an annual budget of $85 million.

- Improved the division's level of service while reducing its operating budget.
- Identified over $30 million cost opportunity improvements within the first 90 days.
- Led successful Y2K business verification for 3,000+ business processes and 250 users across 46 teams.

RANDY CLAPP, *Page Two*

- Led a Corporate Initiation Process for all IS Projects to ensure they delivered value.
- Established a Claims Strategy through the assessment of Oxford's Claims Processing Engines.
- Led a Benchmark Initiative across Oxford's IS infrastructure that identified $15+ million in annual savings.

ELECTRONIC DATA SYSTEMS Pittsburgh, PA   1997–1999

Account Executive supporting EDS' U.S. Banking Strategic Business Unit

Reporting to the President of U.S Banking, led a consulting engagement with Mellon Bank's Software Engineering Department (SED). SED was an organization of 1500+ software professionals and an annual budget of $170 million.

- Helped SED meet three key objectives:
  predictable delivery, time to market, and productivity.
- Enabled project management disciplines within SED and used the Software Engineering Institutes Capability Maturity Model (SEI-CMM) as the yardstick for improvement.
- Identified $17+ million cost opportunity improvements for Mellon Bank within first 6 months.
- Developed a business proposition to save Mellon Bank $274 million over 10 years.
- Created a pipeline of opportunity for EDS valued at $750 million.

ELECTRONIC DATA SYSTEMS Detroit, MI   1993–1997

Account Executive supporting EDS' Diversified Financial Services (DFS) Strategic Business Unit

Reporting to the Vice President of DFS, supported technology solutions for GMAC's Commercial Lending business. Maintained customer relationship valued at $25 million annually for EDS. Other responsibilities included: staff of 150+ professionals, project and financial planning, staffing, organizing, directing and controlling activities of the business.

- Between 1995 and 1997 **tripled revenues while decreasing costs by 30%**.
- Led an organization of 150+ software professionals to SEI-CMM Level 2 compliance.
- Managed the development and **implementation of 300+ projects** for GMACFS.
- Sponsored Software Process Improvement Network and executive committee that **led peer organizations of 800+ professionals** to SEI-CMM Level 2 compliance.
- Identified and implemented a process across peer organizations to **increase profitability by $25M annually**.

RANDY CLAPP, *Page Three*

ELECTRONIC DATA SYSTEMS Dayton, Ohio 1989–1993

Systems Engineering Manager supporting EDS' System Services Strategic Business Unit

Led several application teams that provided technology solutions for three major banking clients. Managed 60 professionals and multi-million dollar project budgets that spanned several months.

- Led an application development team that implemented new systems for a major financial institution's fleet financing business. The development project was 15,000+ function points. Utilized solid project management practices and the **development effort was 400% more productive** than other efforts of similar characteristics.
- Led a Strategic Planning Team that monitored projects throughout their life cycles to ensure target and budget objectives were met, and provided strategic direction in conformance with the client's business goals.
- Project Leader responsible for defining a North American System strategy for GMAC which included defining business rules, designing for flexibility and ease of enhancement, and developing an integrated information base.

Project Manager supporting EDS' System Services Strategic Business Unit

- As a Project Manager, responsible for **leading a project team of 120+ professionals** in the successful implementation of the first credit release of EDS' financial product to three major clients.
- Worked with Corporate Human Resources to **implement a Career Development Portfolio throughout a division of 1,000+ professionals**. The assignment involved customizing tools and processes for the division and training the leadership team in multiple sites across the United States.
- Led the development of a financial product design class that **provided training for 800+ professionals** on the system architecture. The result of this effort was to reduce the learning curve on the project from ten months to less than six weeks.
- As a Project Manager, developed a plan that would sync separate development efforts and a production release into a single release of an EDS financial product across three different clients.

GENERAL MOTORS OF CANADA Toronto, Ontario 1981–1989

Systems Engineer: 8+ years of direct experience designing, coding and implementing systems.

EDUCATION

B.A. in Business Management at Northwood University, Midland Michigan

DEANE R. BARON

22 Stanford Street   home 442-445-4444
Coppell, TX 75019   drb@anywhere.net   mobile 214-554-5555

International Senior Executive

with a unique blend of operations, finance, marketing and business development
in US Government and Global markets in the communications technology sectors.

Mexico   South America   Israel   Australia   Canada

Harvard MBA   Fluent in Spanish

Results
- Turned around declining business by upgrading region team and focusing on growth opportunities, which **tripled sales and improved earnings 8 times in 3 years**.
- Launched new radio product and obtained **GSA Schedule**, US Government certification to **MIL STD specifications** and **endorsement by Homeland Security Agencies**.
- Won **45% US Government market share and $10M+ sales within 2 years** for newly launched radio product line in US Dept of Defense and Homeland Security markets.
- **Won two $500M contracts** for nationwide Mexico wireless networks through superior customer relationships and tailored proposals, beating global competitors.
- **Negotiated $300M+ commercial contracts** with Colombian and Israeli customers and drove receivables down 67% through establishing effective customer relationships.
- Recognized with **Top Leadership Award in Nortel CALA** for superior results building relationships, and improving profitability and cash flow in rapidly growing business.

Expertise

- **P&L Responsibility**
- **Turnaround Leadership**
- **Negotiation Strategies**
- **Partnerships / Alliances**

- **Customer Relationships**
- **Business Development**
- **Marketing Strategies**
- **Financing Strategies**

Recognized For
- *Superior Communication • Leadership • Customer Focus • Team Leadership*
- *Imagination and Creativity • Analytical Judgments • Integrity*

CODAN US, Inc., Manassas, Virginia   2002–2006
Australian public company with $125M global revenue supplying communications equipment in Satellite, HF Radio and Digital Microwave Links markets.
DEANE R. BARON, *Page Two*

Deane R. Baron, *Page Two*

General Manager, Americas
Region Executive for North and South America markets.
- *Grew revenues from $8M to $25M.*
- Launched HF Radio products into US Government market, **exceeded $10M annual sales at highest margins globally.**
- *Won EPA and Dept of Treasury contracts* for domestic backup communications.
- Obtained *GSA Schedule Award* as foreign supplier by setting up final assembly manufacturing in US.
- Obtained *US Government product certification* through testing to MIL STD specifications, and *endorsement by Homeland Security Department agencies*.
- Grew satellite product sales *from $8M to $14M in a flat market*, by upgrading sales and support team, and focusing on relationships with US Dept of Defense.
- Launched links product into Global market, recruited experienced sales professionals, *won projects in 4 countries by developing dealer network*.
- Developed new customer relationship generating $2M offshore business, overcoming aggressive competition from large multi-national vendor.
- *Improved profitability 8×* through growing sales and managing costs.

DRB International, Richardson, Texas   2000–2002
Consulting firm
- As mentor with Startech Early Ventures, supported entrepreneurs to strengthen business plans for early stage financing from first tier VC's.
- Developed and recommended turnaround plan for troubled $50M telecom operator.

NORTEL NETWORKS, *Various locations*   1979–2000
Global leader in wireless Internet and optical telecommunications solutions.

Vice President, Wireless Business Development, Richardson Texas 1999–2000
Set priorities on new wireless opportunities worldwide.
- Increased global market share by 1.5% by winning 55% of major projects awarded.
- Developed global approach to $600M GTE International business.

Vice President, Mexico Wireless, Mexico City, Mexico 1995–1999
As COO, grew business to $200M annually from $50M
- **Won two wireless multi-year contracts worth $1 Billion** for nationwide Mexico deployments, beating out aggressive global players.
- Closed large contracts for Fixed Wireless Access networks by **developing close working relationships with customers**, beating Lucent, Ericsson and Nera, despite less favorable offer for customer financing.

DEANE R. BARON, *Page Three*

Vice President, Mexico Wireless, Mexico City, Mexico 1995–1999 (continued)
- *Tailored network solution to unique customer needs*, integrating 3rd party billing system, civil works and wireless telephones into wireless network proposal, and co-coordinating team members in Mexico City, Dallas and Miami.
- *Boosted employee satisfaction from 71% to 80%* in uncertain business environment through *effective team communication*, including in Spanish language.

Director, Marketing Operations, Miami, Florida, 1993–1995
Developed commercial relationships, led supply chain management and logistics / distribution for wireless business in Lain America and Israel.
- Supported business unit growth *from $100M to $250M revenue over two years*.
- *Negotiated $300M+ multi-year equipment supply contracts* with 4 new customers in Colombia and in Israel, including 3 contracts in the Spanish language.
- *Secured $7M Brazil Foreign Exchange Gains* by negotiating and implementing new documentation process with Brazil partner that accelerated collections and repatriation of funds.
- *Reduced receivables by 67%* in Days Sales Outstanding through close operating relationships with existing and new customers.

CFO, Nortel Cala (Caribbean & Latin America), Miami, Florida,   **1989–1993**
- <u>Arranged $110M medium term Latin America customer financing</u> for new business annually, growing from $100M to $250M.
- <u>Strengthened relationships with key Export Credit Agencies</u> in Canada and USA to proactively support key customers.
- Integrated best processes of both parent companies in <u>managing Joint Venture between Motorola and Nortel as CALA CFO</u>, including new proposal evaluation and approval process.

Prior Professional Experience

Various Marketing and Finance Leadership Roles.	1979–1989
Harvard Business School	1977–1979
Procter & Gamble, Hamilton, Canada	1976–1977

Education

MBA, Harvard Business School, 1979
B.A. Sc., Mechanical Engineering, University of Waterloo, 1976—top 1% of class

Table 2 Response To an Ad: Two Formats

John Smith

October 21st, 2006
Ms. Sylvia Malarn
Human Resources Manager
ABC Systems, Inc.
Rome, Italy

Dear Ms. Malarn:
I am applying for the Director of Professional Services position in Italy, Job ID: FM070502. Below I have summarized your key requirements for the position with my matching qualifications:

KEY REQUIREMENTS	MY QUALIFICATIONS
• Leverage, drive, and be responsible for Professional Services delivery in Italy	• Drove $20M+ in incremental revenue and add-on business. • $7.8M at 35%+ margin in outsourcing solutions. • Oversaw more than 100 projects and several delivery teams, from pre-sale to implementation to post-production.
• Develop high level customer relationships	• Interfaced with senior management in many Fortune 500 companies, including delivering presentations at sales meetings. • Many of our largest clients insisted I attend their strategic planning discussions. • Interacted daily with C-level executives at Pacer Logistics including the Division President, and Controller to steer a $2M enterprise application implementation.
• Work with a compatible partner ecosystem; Business Developer and Performer	• Created innovative technology and service partnerships to augment Sterling's suite of offerings and improve service delivery. • Identified and negotiated partner deal with a customs broker to provide interfaces to U.S. Customs' Automated Commercial Environment, enabling new revenue and minimizing investment.
• Project Management	• 7 years of project management, with PMI training. • Currently a consulting project manager at a logistics client, leading a $2M enterprise application project with a 30+ person team through structured SLDC development processes.

Please call to further discuss the details of my business experience: 614-222-8585 (USA). I am fully open to relocation and frequent travel.

Sincerely,

John Smith
Encl: Résumé
For the vertical format the same letter would look like this:

John Smith

October 21st, 2006

Ms. Sylvia Malarn
Human Resources Manager
ABC Systems, Inc.
Rome, Italy

Dear Ms. Malarn:

I am applying for the Director of Professional Services position in Italy, Job ID: FM070502. Below I have summarized your key requirements for the position with my matching qualifications:

1. **Your key requirement**: "Leverage, drive, and be responsible for Professional Services delivery in Italy."
   My qualifications:
   - Drove $20M+ in incremental revenue and add-on business.
   - $7.8M at 35%+ margin in outsourcing solutions.
   - Oversaw more than 100 projects and several delivery teams, from pre-sale to implementation to post-production.

2. **Your key requirement**: "Develop high level customer relationships."
   My qualifications:
   - Interfaced with senior management in many Fortune 500 companies, including delivering presentations at sales meetings.
   - Many of our largest clients insisted I attend their strategic planning discussions.
   - Interacted daily with C-level executives at Pacer Logistics including the Division President, and Controller to steer a $2M enterprise application implementation.

TIP: If you aren't comfortable creating tables the vertical format is recommended and is equally effective.

Table 3 Cover Letter for Retained Search Firm Specializing in Your Target Market

ABC Retained Search
444 Broadway
Anytown, USA

Dear Bob,

I am a senior marketing executive in the nanotechnology field, most recently as SVP of Marketing at Zeon Instruments, a $250M leader in scientific instruments for the nanotechnology sector. Prior to that was the VP Sales at ABC Instruments, a $100M company providing microscopes for analyzing materials at the atomic scale.

At Zeon Instruments
- Introduced the first web based product launch in the company's history targeting the top 1000 senior scientists in the US, Russia and Europe.
- Sales were 150% of plan in the first six months.
- Increased worldwide market share an average of 18% across five major product lines.

ABC Instruments
- Exceeded revenue plan five years in a row.
- Provided the sales leadership that enabled the business to grow from $10M to $100M in five years.

My goal is to remain in nanotechnology.

My total cash compensation at Zeon was $228k as well as an equity position.

I am open to relocation.

My résumé is attached.

Sincerely,
J. W. Scope

Table 7 Cover Letter for a Named Search Firm Specializing in Your Target Market

6
...

Is Networking Motherhood? *This Question Is Easy To Answer. No!*

Chapter Overview ....

- The Five O'Clock Club definition of networking
- Why making direct contacts will improve your odds
- Networking do's and don'ts
- A technique guaranteed to expand your network by at least 50 contacts

....

The Difference Between Networking and Direct Contact

For decades the data hasn't changed and the data says the vast majority of senior level jobs are obtained through either **networking** or **direct contact**.

Networking, however, is defined too broadly by most people. And for them it means contact with anybody! At the Five O'Clock Club we like to be a bit more precise.

Networking is either contacting people you know or using someone's name to connect with someone else. It is not just a technique, but a process. It is a process of building long lasting relationships. Merely calling for information will never build a strong network.

Successful networkers share as much information as they receive. In fact, Harvey Mackay in his excellent book on networking, *Dig Your Well Before You Are Thirsty*, says "the best networkers are the best givers."

Direct Contact is also a very powerful tool frequently overlooked and underutilized. It is when you write or call someone you do not know. Let us give you a compelling reason for adding this technique to your job search arsenal.

In the most recent Five O'Clock Club survey we found executives got 30% of their interviews through **direct contact**. We will talk more about this technique in the next chapter.

Networking is also more than a job search tool. It is a powerful process of acquiring and sharing knowledge through successful interactions with others, at all levels. These interactions will enable you to advance your learning, stimulate your career, help you to benchmark your leadership skills, provide valuable input to complex business or life balance issues as well as uncover the best contractor to remodel your house or kitchen. We believe choosing to be a good networker is a life-style decision.

Now all this is great in theory but how do you realistically do it when you don't seem to have enough hours in the day to get through your top priorities?

We will discuss three scenarios:

1. Networking when things are going well, green light mode.
2. When there are a few clouds on the horizon, yellow light mode.
3. When it is time to leave, red light mode.

Networking . . . In Green-Light Mode.

In green light mode things are going well so your networking efforts should concentrate on longer term career goals, staying in touch with the thought leaders in your industry and keeping up on global trends. And while there never seem to be enough hours in the day to do this here are some practical tips:

- Have a realistic, written game plan. Written because it creates more of a commitment and realistic so you won't get discouraged. For example, scheduling two or three breakfasts a month should be very realistic. We say breakfast because lunches have the highest cancellation rate.

- Who should these breakfasts be with? One should be with an industry expert. One should be with someone who can impact your career either by being able to hire you or introduce you to someone who could hire you. The third is with people you just want to stay connected with. These could be friends, peers, or old bosses. Notice we didn't suggest meeting with an executive recruiter. You know the buzz that happens when someone sees you meeting publicly with a head hunter. The rumor mill goes into full swing and it is seldom positive. However, it is important to stay in touch with a few top flight executive recruiters but best to do that over the phone.
- Phone and email are also effective ways to stay in touch. They can and should be done in the off hours, off hours being defined as before 8AM and after 6PM. We suggest you target just one or two of these calls a week.
- Also don't forget to give your time to people who need it. Return those networking phone calls. A few minutes of your time could mean a lot to somebody. And when it is your time to ask for help, **they will remember**.

We want you to stop and think for just a moment. If you followed the above game plan and were successful 75% of the time during the year, how strong would your network be? How confident would you be about your knowledge of key trends, the job market as well as your market value?

The good news is to do it well takes only five or six hours a month and none of these hours are coming from your prime time or your family time.

Networking . . . In Yellow Light Mode.

In yellow-light mode there are some clouds at the horizon. There may have been an unexpected reorganization, a new boss, a significant downsizing or bad financial results.

You need to take charge and networking is one of your most powerful tools to help you learn more about the situation and develop personal strategies. Here the time commitment jumps to at least four to five hours a week. Our suggestions:

- Start networking within your own organization to understand who has more knowledge than you do about the situation or who can directly or indirectly influence it. Think about who the key decision makers and influencers are.
- More than ever, you need to attend company gatherings. They can be great places to tap into the informal organization.
- Stay around for a little after important meetings so you can chat.

- Have coffee with key peers.
- Volunteer for cross-functional or cross-divisional projects, they are a great way to network into other parts of your organization.
- Attend relevant training programs, these are a great way to network inside your organization.
- Immediately start to network outside your organization. Focus on the people and organizations that know your company well such as customers or clients, suppliers, industry experts, industry association members, former colleagues and former bosses who have left the company. Schedule phone calls or meetings with them to see what their perceptions are about your company and you.
- Pick a group of trusted friends and colleagues to ask what they would do in your situation and to brainstorm possible next steps.

Networking . . . In Red Light Mode.

In a red-light mode you may have been asked to leave, or the performance of the business is such that you know it is only a matter of time and you have to make a full court press. The first people you should reach out to:

- The smartest people you know in the industry
- People whose career you admire and would like to emulate
- The most connected people
- Bosses you worked well with
- Trusted executive recruiter(s)
- Your significant other and family members
- Your best friend(s)

Networking Do's and Don'ts

Here is a quick list of what to do and what to avoid as you crank up your network. What to do . . . and these are "musts."

- **Do reconnect** with **everyone** you have lost touch with and we mean **everyone**. And please don't tell us you don't know where they are. That old saw "six degrees of separation" has now dropped to "three degrees of separation" in the 21st Century. So with a few phone calls or a few "Googles" you should be able to track down most anyone out there.

Among the most common concerns we hear around the "reconnecting" theme are gut issues such as, "what do I say?" or "I feel so guilty."

Here is what you do first, think about the last time someone out of your past called you after a number of years. How did it feel? Wasn't it almost instantly like they had never been out of touch? Well guess what? It is going to be exactly the same when they hear from you. **They will be delighted!**

Another "excuse" we hear is, all of my good contacts are retired. First, retired executives seldom really retire. Ask their families! We find while they may be playing a bit more golf or tennis, most stay very active. They often maintain one or two Board seats or are seriously involved in the not-for-profit sector. This means **they still have active networks**.

- **Always come bearing gifts**. As we have all read many times, effective networking is a two way street. So what gift do you bring? Well it is not "a box with a ribbon around it" gift but simply a current article or piece of news about something they are personally interested in. It can be about their company or a company they use to work for, it can be about their profession, their hobby or something you know they are passionate about.

The important don'ts.

- **Don't be a pest**. Not that anyone reading this book would ever fall into that category! The best way to avoid being perceived as a pest is to follow one of the Five O'Clock Club principles which is, after your first voice mail . . . do not leave any other messages. However you can still be "seen" (literally) if you also don't block "caller ID." So please check with your friendly phone company on how to do that. For example, in the US you punch in *67 and your name and number will not appear on the caller ID of the person you are calling and *82 to unlock for another call where caller ID is no longer an issue.

    Many of you are now asking yourself, then how the heck do I ever get to a real person? Good question. We call it "bracketed calling" and it works like a charm especially for Type-A executives. You start calling earlier and earlier in the day and later and later in the evening. Sooner or later they will pick up. Remember the times you were in the office at 7AM and the phone rang? The first thing that runs through your mind is, who on earth would be calling at this hour? Right? We have all been there. And most of the time we couldn't resist picking up the phone just to satisfy our curiosity. It is not unusual to make 10–12 calls before reaching a live person and we have had some clients that have reported making 30. The lesson: Good old persistence will pay off.

- **Don't let your network get stale.** You should keep your name in front of your Stage-1 contacts every month. In Chapter 8 we will cover the three Stages of a job search but basically your Stage-1 contacts are the people you want to stay in touch with throughout your search. They know you well and are in a position to either hire you or recommend you to someone who can hire you.

One of the best ways to stay in touch to send them "gifts" as we discussed above. A tip on how to stay on top of this is to use the calendar reminder in your contact manager. For example in Outlook it is the little red flag on the contact record. So all you have to do, after sending an article or if you just talked to them, is type in the next date you want to check in and your system will automatically remind you on that date as soon as you turn on your computer.

How to Quickly Add 50 to 200 Names to Your Network?

We will give you a sure fire way to add a minimum of 50 names to your network. Some of our clients have completed this exercise and ended up adding as many as 200 names.

First we encourage you to **take off your networking blinders**. The biggest blinders fall into three areas:

1. **The functional or industry "blinders."**

This is where you only network with people from your functional area(s) of expertise or only those who have worked in your industry.

A classic example is someone in finance not calling someone in marketing or sales. It is almost as if no one in marketing or sales would know anyone in finance. And of course when you think about it rationally it is kind of silly. The same is true with the industry blinder. Why would I talk to anyone in healthcare about high tech?

The bottom line is you are looking to talk to people who know people. We agree in the beginning of your search it may make sense to prioritize this way but you need to quickly branch out without the blinders. Rationally you know some one in Healthcare can have lots of contacts in high tech and visa versa. They could be married to an executive in high tech, they might have worked in high tech themselves in a previous life. Their best friend is an executive in high tech. Well . . . you get the point.

2. The relatives "blinder."

What we usually hear from our clients is, why on earth would I call my Aunt Mary? She hasn't worked a day in her life.

Well let's give you a true Aunt Mary story. One of our clients begrudgingly agreed to call some of her relatives after we coached her on networking. Guess what? Her Aunt Mary ended up introducing her to one of the most senior female executives at a well know high-tech company. What was the connection? Aunt Mary played bridge with the executive's Mom. So dust off your list of relatives and let them know what and who you are targeting.

3. Your Alumni "blinder "

Almost 70% of executives have failed to contact their Alumni office(s). This is crazy!

Every alum who is in the alumni office data base has had to agree, formally, to allow either students or alumni or both to contact them. This almost guarantees a return call. The other great thing about the majority of alumni databases is they are searchable. So if you are targeting HP or Home Depot you can look for all the alumni from your school who work there. Talk about focus! This is truly a networking gold mine.

Now let's look at how you can easily add 50 to 200 new names to your networking list. We call it "rescrubbing your network."

- Think about all the clubs you and your family belong to besides the usual country, tennis or yacht clubs. Spend some time thinking about the less traditional clubs like the coin, stamp, bridge, poker, book or antique clubs.
- Review your holiday card list plus your family and business email list. While this is nothing new we find very few of our clients have really sat down and thoroughly gone through them and then made calls. If anyone on those lists does not know you are in transition or who or what your targets are then you are doing yourself a disservice.
- How about all those sororities and fraternities you and the family have belonged to?
- How about neighbors especially the ones you prejudged like the 80-year-old widower who doesn't appear to have many friends but if you chatted with her you would find her grandson is now an SVP at Microsoft?
- How about the parents of your children's best friends? How many can you reach out to? The same goes with the sports teams you and the family are (or

have been) involved in. We bet most of the parents are professionals or executives like you.

- Have you thought about sharing your target list with your doctor(s), dentist(s), barber or hair stylist? We had one client who mentioned one of his target companies to his barber and the barber said, "I cut that CEO's hair." He went on to say he would personally hand the CEO the guy's résumé the next time he was in.
- Think about all the professional people you do business with such as your accountant, family attorney, real estate broker, banker, insurance agent or stock broker. Their client list may contain the key executive you are trying to connect with.
- From your business life please think about:
  ✓ Vendors, suppliers, sales people who called on you
  ✓ Third-party leasing companies
  ✓ All consultants you have used
  ✓ Dust off those attendee lists from seminars or conferences you have attended
  ✓ Don't forget your company's competitors
  ✓ Fund raising campaigns you were involved with
  ✓ VC's you have dealt with
  ✓ Business banking contacts
- From your educational life please think about:
  ✓ Your grade school, high school and college buddies. You will find it triggers a number of people you would like to reconnect with.
  ✓ We talked about connecting with the Alumni Office but you also want to contact your Alumni Association(s). They often have excellent networking events.
  ✓ Adult education classes you have attended
  ✓ Now for all of these educational contacts you have gone through for yourself, do the same thing with your kids (especially your adult aged children), wife, husband, or significant other
  TIP: This tactic alone could double or triple your network list.
- From your community life please think about:
  ✓ The Mayor and counsel members
  ✓ PTA

✓ The Chamber of Commerce
✓ Community fund raisers
✓ Girl Scouts and Boy Scouts
✓ Community organizations you or the family have been involved in

For Those Who Think They Don't Have a Network . . . A Case Study

Jean, a successful marketing executive, had been out of the workforce for five years taking care of her twin boys. Far from being idle, she had leveraged her MBA and track record in marketing working as a volunteer for a not-for-profit company working out of her home.

When she decided to return to the workforce, she worked with us to uncover her primary job target: marketing consulting companies in the Atlantic Region.

Then Jean got discouraged. She felt having been out the workforce for five years would be a major drawback, especially since networking and direct contact would be her primary means for getting interviews. When we asked her how big her network was she said maybe 10 people . . . and not even in the right industry!

We told her nicely we didn't believe that for a minute and challenged her to do a little networking audit. We said, "Jean, the first thing you need to do is think about family, friends, business associates, social acquaintances, alums and everyone you have met as a volunteer for the not-for-profit."

Our challenge worked. It was as if we told her she couldn't run a 5k and she would do anything to prove us wrong. She came up with over 350 names!

Here is a list of her sources. Some are obvious others were highly creative.

- Last year's Christmas mailing list
- The invitation list to her fortieth birthday party
- The Alumni office at her graduate school
- The Alumni office at her husband's graduate school
- Her son's elementary school directory
- She combed her Rolodex for all those business cards stuck in there
- She even thought about all the cocktail parties she had attended over the last year and who she connected with
- She pulled out the list of the board members of the not-for-profit she was working for.
- She dug around and found the phone directory for the last company she

worked for. She realized the majority of her contacts would have moved on but used Google to track them down.

The Golden Rules of Networking

1. Be patient. Please remember, your networking calls are strategic not tactical unless you are in Red-Light mode.
2. The key to building a strong long-term network is your ability to develop relationships.
3. Maintain contact, at least quarterly, with everyone who has contributed to your learning and growth over the years.
4. Ask for advice and support, as opposed to favors.
5. Focus on those who have spontaneously given to you.
6. Try to always bring a "gift" to the table. It can be something as simple as a current article about their company or their hobby.
7. Graciously let go of any networking relationship where you are the only one giving.
8. Become a mentor for at least two people you believe have potential.

Chapter Summary ·

Our clients have found that if they "re-scrubbed" their networks, they always managed to add at lease 50 names and sometimes hundreds.

• Send copies of your Marketing Plan to your network. It allows them to laser focus on your targeted companies.
• And remember, direct contact is a terrific way to supplement your networking. The last Five O'Clock study showed executives got 30% of their interviews through direct contact.

7
•••

A No Nonsense Approach To Interviewing

Chapter Overview ··

- Real data on how executives get interviews
- Why direct contact and direct mail are important
- Why the results from ads and executive recruiters are so lousy
- The seven keys to successful interviewing
- Doing "due diligence" or **before you say yes** to any job offer . . . check out the new boss and the new culture **very** carefully

···

How Do Executives Actually Get Interviews?

Ask most executives about the methods they used when they looked for a job and they are likely to tell you networking, executive search firms, and ads. Rarely do they mention direct contact. Well, in 2005, our COO, Richard Bayer decided to do a formal survey of Five O'Clock Club executive clients and his findings were an eye opener.

Nearly 30% got their first meeting by contacting executives directly . . . **without a referral.**

Here is a summary of those findings:

➤ 62% got their interviews through networking

➤ *30% through direct contact*

➤ 5% through executive recruiters

➤ 3% through ads

As we mentioned in the last chapter, **direct contact** is a very powerful but under-utilized tool. It is important because it could lead to 30% of your interviews. Please try it!

Direct Contact and Direct Mail.

Direct Contact . . . Who To Contact?

Contact key decision makers *or influencers* for one of your target companies.

The influencers are the people decision-makers listen to irrespective of their position in the company. At the CEO level the obvious key influencers are the CFO and the heads of sales and marketing. The less obvious influencers are the company's top major account reps or that supervisor in accounts payable who has been with the company for 30 years and knows where all the skeletons are.

A good first move is not to contact the CEO but one of the key direct reports. Also important are Board Members and Executive Committee Members as well as Industry thought leaders.

There could also be other executives, senior level consultants or academics in your target industry you want to contact first. They are valuable on a number of fronts. They can share where they see the industry going, who they see as the emerging stars, which companies are having troubles, as well as insights about the key players and influencers in your target companies.

Where do you find them?

• Start on the target company's website. Many websites include the names and profiles of the senior officers, Board Members, and Executive Committee members.

• Check the membership lists of your professional associations.

• Review Industry directories. Hit the library and talk to the Research Librarian.

- Contact college and grad school alumni offices and don't forget your spouse, significant other or your children's alumni offices.

Direct Contact . . . How to Contact?

One of the quickest is to pick up the phone and call, providing you have your script prepared. The script can be as simple as a few notes "on the back of an envelope" or an actual script you draft on a Word document. The most important thing to script are your opening lines and the lines need to be compelling. They might sound like this: "John, I just read in today's WSJ your comments about building plants in China and they really resonated with me because I just returned from China on an assignment for Ford. Do you have a minute to chat?" Also think of two or three objectives for the call and something you can do for the direct contact. In this example the caller would share what she learned about manufacturing in China. It could also include other appropriate articles on the subject to draw his attention to.

The other part of your **direct contact** strategy is **direct mail**. Like direct contact, direct mail is also underutilized even though independent studies show over **20% of all jobs are found through direct-mail campaigns**.

A Direct and Targeted-Mail Campaign . . . How To Do It Right.

"Mass mailing" often has a negative connotation. The Five O'Clock Club's approach is more thoughtful. We will outline the differences between a direct-mail and targeted-mail campaign, then walk you through the suggested format for the letters.

A Targeted-Mail Campaign . . . A Customized Approach.

This is a limited mailing to approximately 20 of your targets. The qualities of a targeted mailing are:

1. You have done enough research on a company and the decision maker to write a customized letter.
2. This is a letter you are going to personally follow-up on.

A Direct-Mail Campaign . . . A General Approach.

This technique is used when you want to reach a large number (200) of your targets quickly. A targeted mailing is time consuming but highly effective. To reach a larger number of targets, a direct-mail campaign can be an effective tool also.

1. This is not a customized letter but it is written to a decision-maker.
2. A direct-mail campaign could target 60 to 200 people.
3. It must address the issues in your target market. For example if you were doing a direct-mail campaign geared to the storage technology market you would refer specifically to the challenges and opportunities in that market.
4. You do not follow up on your direct-mail letters.

Cover Letter Format

One of the first questions we are often asked is, should I include my résumé? We have a very practical answer: Yes, if it helps your case. Direct-mail experts have found the more enclosures the greater the response rate so unless your recent experiences are problematic we suggest you include your resume.

Another key advantage of the cover letter is you can focus the reader exactly where you want them to focus. With just your résumé, you are never quite sure where they will focus.

First Paragraph . . . Be sure to write **The Grabber**!

Your opening paragraph should immediately engage the reader. It must be targeted to their concerns. Dramatic statistics are often used, but avoid hyperbole. Avoid the "Do you need someone who can . . . (leap tall buildings)?" introduction.

In a targeted mailing, **The Grabber** might start like this:

You recently announced you are building your first plant in Brazil. I thought you might be interested in my experiences with HP, in Brazil, where I opened two manufacturing plants in 18 months utilizing 100% Nationals and achieved 95% retention in the first year.

A direct-mailing opening to companies who may or may not have a South American presence, might start like this:

Businesses expanding into South America and Mexico are always looking for creative ways to maximize the use of Nationals and maintain high retention. I thought you might be interested in my experiences with HP, in Brazil and Mexico. In Brazil I opened two manufacturing plants in 18 months utilizing 100% nationals and had 95% retention in the first year. Prior to that I lived in Mexico for three years, working for Ford, where we built an auto parts manufacturing plant.

Second Paragraph . . . **Your Background.**

This can be as simple as the summary statement off your résumé. It might start like this:

For the last 10 years I have been leading international consumer products launches and penetrating new markets in North America, South America and the Far East, most recently as SVP Global Marketing for P&G.

Third Paragraph . . . **Your Key Accomplishments.**

Gear this to your target market. It can be in paragraph or bullet format. We prefer bullets because the eye can scan them so much quicker. They also need to include the numbers. You want at least 4–6 hard hitting accomplishments. Here are several from our Five O'Clock Club clients:

- **Turned around a declining business** by upgrading the region team and focusing on growth opportunities. We **tripled sales and improved earnings 8-fold times in 3 years**.
- **Won two $500M contracts** for a nationwide Mexico wireless network through superior customer relationships and tailored proposals, beating out global competitors.

The Fourth Paragraph . . . is optional.

Be sure to mention any unique aspects of your background. This could include special leadership roles outside of your company, language expertise, or living in other countries. Mention these factors only when it will benefit your target market.

Final Paragraph . . . How to Close or Follow-up.

A Targeted-Mailing Close:

I will be calling your assistant to set up a convenient time to share my experiences in Brazil.

A Direct-Mailing Close:

I understand how busy you are so I will not bother your office with a follow-up call. However, I trust you will give me a call if you think it would be helpful for us to discuss my experiences in Brazil and Mexico.

A Unique Targeted-Mailing Case Study

One of our clients wrote this Targeted letter to the decision maker **after** she answered their ad. She tracked down who the hiring manager was and wrote him directly. The hiring manager was impressed enough to ask HR to pull her résumé out of the stack and she was interviewed within a few days.

Here is the letter she wrote:

Dear Mr. Glover,

I recently applied to the VP Strategy position that you advertised on your website.

It is my understanding that one of the objectives of this position will be to simplify the product line for long-lasting cost savings and future growth.

I am currently a Director of Strategy with ABC Inc. A quick recap of my background:

- International project leader with 8 years of experience in Operational Strategy, Supply Chain and Change Management in Consumer Products.
- Recently led the development and implementation of a Post Merger global optimization program in North America, with expected savings of 15% for 140 sites across the world.
- Have bicultural experience in North America, Europe, Australia and Brazil, leading multi-cultural and multi-functional teams.
- Fluent in English, French and Portuguese.

I would like to talk to you about my qualifications for this position. I will call your assistant at the end of the week to arrange a mutually convenient time for a discussion.

Enclosed is the résumé I submitted along with my application for your reference.

Best regards,

Nathan Powell

Why Are The Response Rates For Ads And Executive Recruiters So Low?

"It's a little chilly in here. Throw another batch of résumés we have on file in the fire."

The numbers are low because companies traditionally try networking and employee referrals first. And while our survey showed only an 8% response rate for executive recruiters and ads they are still two very viable channels. They can also be leveraged to enhance your research, your network, and could be the direct path to a great job.

CAUTION: Just make sure the time you invest in these two areas is roughly proportional to the response rate percentage which means spending no more than 8–10% of your search time in these areas.

Executive Recruiters

When we say "**executive recruiter**" we are talking about **retained search firms only**. The retained search firm gets paid even if the company decides not to hire. The contingency firm is paid "contingent" on the company hiring someone. There are some fine contingency recruiters out there but your focus should be primarily on retained search firms.

One of the most frequent complaints we hear is "I never get a response when I send an unsolicited résumé to an executive recruiter." If they don't have a current search that matches your exact profile you probably won't hear from them. Does that mean it's not worth the effort? Absolutely not. An experienced, savvy executive recruiter can become an important partner in your job search and there are several techniques that may get you a phone call.

Let's look at how the retained search business model works and some tips on how to get recognized by retained search firms.

1. As you know, their loyalty is to their client . . . the company that is paying them.

2. Executive recruiters, more often than not, are hired to find the "needle in the haystack" candidate.

    Think about the last time you used an executive recruiter. You probably did not call them until you had exhausted your own network and your HR department's network. You also probably ran some ads, posted it internally and on a few job boards.

3. Executive recruiters have little room for creativity as they network for candidates. Their clients, who have decided to spend serious dollars on an executive search, want the perfect candidate who meets all the specs. As we mentioned, if your résumé does not exactly match the specs you will not be considered.

4. Executive recruiters only tap into the pool of unsolicited résumés after they have exhausted their networks and direct contacts.

5. This is always tough to swallow but the majority of companies also want someone who is currently employed. Have they gotten a little more flexible? Yes, but only marginally.

So how do you get their attention?

1. Select executive recruiters who are going to be interested in you. This means you have hired them in the past, you are likely to hire them in the future or you are a recognized name in the industries they specialize in.

2. Find out from your business network the best firms in your functional area or market. If you are a CFO in Healthcare find out who the best are in these areas. This is just like finding the best pediatricians or physicians.

3. Once you have the names of a few recruiters find out if any of your close business contacts have used them. Then, with their permission, use their name in your introductory paragraph to the recruiter. This is one of the most effective ways to get a call back especially if your opening is not just "Jane Smith suggested I contact you." You want to let them know how well you know Jane and that you had a "very interesting" discussion about their search firm. An approach like this will almost always result in a call because their curiosity is killing them.

4. A totally different approach is to send a cover letter where you treat them as an industry expert. Ask them for a few minutes to discuss the sector(s) they are expert in. At the same time highlight your own level and describe your targets and attach an interesting industry publication.

What if an executive recruiter does call?

1. First, find out if they are networking or they are targeting you. If they are targeting you and the job isn't a fit, help the recruiter by giving them referrals. This is the best way to start a relationship. Also take advantage of the call to get their insights into your target markets.

2. Find out as quickly as you can the name of the company for which they are recruiting and if it is a retained search. If it is a contingency search you do not want to be a candidate for a position where you have already made contact. If it is a retained search and you realize it is a position you have already had conversations about make sure you let the recruiter know. This will build trust. Also let the decision maker know you received a call. You need to understand why they decided to go to retained search rather than hire you directly. It is a great opportunity to ask the hiring manager how they view your candidacy and if there is anything about your experience that is a concern.

3. What if the position or company they are calling about is not really of high interest but it is at the right level, in the right function and in the right industry? We believe it makes sense to explore it for several reasons. First, you will establish a relationship with the recruiter, second you will meet some potentially valuable executive contacts, and last your perception of the job or company just might change as a result of the meeting.

How Do You Navigate the Job-Ad Ocean On the Internet?

A Little Background.

Ads are a rich source of information about market and job trends. More and more executive jobs are being advertised because executive search is costly. The other trend is the move to predominantly online ads, either on the company website or major job boards or both.

When we say "ocean" we aren't exaggerating. At the time this book was written there were over 30,000 job boards!

Prioritizing

- Your first source should be your target companies' websites. Most companies have a career section where current jobs are posted.
- Your second source is executive job banks. Some job boards have reached worldwide recognition, such as Monster.com, but the job board landscape changes almost daily. So how do you wade through the morass of job boards and stay on top of new ones? It's easy. Just use your favorite search engine, like Google, and do the following queries:
  - ✦ "Best executive job sites for IT."
  - ✦ "Best executives sites in biotech."
  - ✦ "Best executive job board aggregators." (We got over 300k hits when we tried this.) Aggregators sweep multiple boards so it is a more efficient way of searching.

    One example of an aggregator is **Indeed** (www.indeed.com). They sweep over 500 websites including Monster, Career Builder, Hot Jobs and Career Mole. They also sweep the top 200 newspapers, hundreds of associations and company sites.
  - ✦ Or just "best job boards." (We found over 67 million hits when we did this.)

The Seven Keys to Successful Interviewing

One of the major mistakes interviewers make is trying to close the deal on the first interview. How many times have you heard people say, when they learn you were going on your first interview, "we hope you get the job!" At the Five O Clock Club, we say, "we hope you don't!" because it is totally unrealistic when you think about it. You can't possibly learn enough to make such a serious decision based upon a few hours of discussion.

1. Understand and Internalize The Purpose of the First Interview. It is simply, to give and get enough information that leads to a second interview.

2. "Think And Act" Like a Consultant.

Adopt a mindset that you are the worlds best consultant. You have no stake in the outcome of this meeting. You are not trying to land an assignment. You are only there to tell them what is right for this organization, not what is right for you.

3. Preparation . . . Preparation . . . Preparation.

Professional musicians rehearse and rehearse, and then rehearse some more. They practice until the fingering of their instrument or breathing is automatic. They practice until they can play it without thinking about it and can just feel it. Daniel Goleman

It is exactly the same for pulling off successful interviews.

Think about your preparation for a job interview just as you would for preparing for a presentation to the executive committee, board or major client. Leave no stone unturned.

Here are the steps to follow for great preparation before every first round of interviews. These steps are also great insurance against your competition outshining you.

Research your target thoroughly. (This is a good time to re-read Chapter 4.)

In summary, research using the library, the internet, your network, analysts' reports, and other public data about your target company and its key executives.

It is the same process you would use if you were doing an analysis of your top competitor(s) for a Board presentation. Chances are you and your team would do some form of SWOT analysis looking at their Strengths, Weaknesses, Opportunities and Threats.

Part of your research is to consult with the experts. A few examples: the journalist who has recently interviewed the executive(s) you are targeting, an academic or consultant who has worked with the company, or a major presenter at a recent industry conference.

Research the people you will be meeting with. Easy to do in today's internet world. Just "Google" them! Other resources are the 10K's and 10Q's, *The Ward Directory for Private Companies* and if you have access to LexusNexus plug in everyone's name you are interviewing with. LexusNexus searches all the times they have been in the press and gives you access to the actual articles. A powerful tool to have going into an interview and it will put you ahead of your competition, unless they have read this book too!

Often overlooked: Ask everyone in your network if they know any of the key players. It can be a simple email: "Mary, do you know Lynn Smith EVP Operations at ABC, Inc.?"

One more time, check your **alumni office** to see if any alums work there and call them all before the interview.

Don't be afraid to be bold and creative. One of our clients, a senior marketing director, even paid for a focus group to better understand market trends in a new market segment. Yes, this is a bit over the top, but doing it gave him a **breakthrough idea** on how the company could penetrate a new market. And yes, he got the job.

4. Tell Great Stories.

Good interviewers craft stories that highlight their accomplishments and at the same time are directly related to the client needs.

We had a client who was interviewing with a Mexican company so he made sure he told "stories" about all his Mexican experiences. These included how he went about developing his network in the Mexican business community, how he successfully entered a new market and how much he enjoyed living in Mexico for three years.

A good way to frame your stories is first to talk about all the unique challenges you faced, then how you and your team met the challenges and last the punch line, your results.

TIPS: **Always credit the Team** and use lots of "we's" and no "I's."

5. Prepare For the Tough Questions.

We define tough questions simply as "any question you hope they don't ask."
While we can't cover all the tough questions for you personally we can share some of the common themes.

- Short tenure with a company
- Frequent job changes
- Any gap in employment
- Compensation that is well above or well below the market
- Why you left each company
- Any performance that was below plan
- What your boss would criticize you for

Guidelines for answering the tough questions.

- Do not try and "spin" your answer. Think about how you reacted the last time someone was giving you a "spun" answer. Here is the classic "spun" answer to, "why did you leave?" "Well there was a reorganization and my unit was eliminated."

    Tell them the truth. If someone else got the job you should have had say that without being critical of your competitor or company. In fact, compliment whenever you can. It demonstrates class. The right response, "spin-free" would be something like, "the CEO thought Janet had more product launch experience and she did."

- Practice your answers to tough questions with your coach, mentors and trusted friends. We have several executive clients who meet regularly whenever they are about to go on interviews and they practice on each other.

- Change your mindset about tough questions. Think of them as great questions and an opportunity to tell a short story about your learning process and personal growth.

    Tough questions also offer insights into the culture and style of your potential boss, peers and direct reports. What if the interviewers keep asking if you have had experience firing people? This might be an early warning sign of what you will be up against.

6. Ask Great Questions.

Everyone focuses on the potential questions the interviewers will be asking but unfortunately to the exclusion of thinking about, "what questions should I be asking?" Guidelines for great questions:

- First, they need to be tough questions but asked in a nice way. A good mind set is one of a Wall Street analyst but again with a soft touch not a club.

  Put all that excellent research you have just completed to good use; Why has the cost of sales been increasing (for three quarters in a row)? Why did you take $10M out of R&D last year?

- Great questions should validate the following:
  - ✦ Two or three key deliverables they expect from you and the time lines for each
  - ✦ Any objection to you as a viable candidate
  - ✦ How you stack up against your competition
  - ✦ The potential for career growth
  - ✦ Cultural fit with the company and your potential boss
  - ✦ And most important, will your strengths and experience allow you to exceed their expectations?

- How to avoid sounding like a prosecuting attorney.

  The style and delivery of your questions will make all the difference here. Above we said a good mind set is one of a Wall Street analyst with a soft touch. What does a soft touch sound like? For example, asking why the cost of sales have gone up is an appropriate question but delivered with a soft touch it would sound more like, "I noticed your cost of sales has been going up, is that by design?" Another way to soften your questions is to begin with, **"may I ask** what has been driving up your cost of sales?" Or, what were the factors behind reducing R&D?

  The softer touch allows you to get at critical issues without putting the interviewer on the defensive.

7. Do Great Follow-up.

At the Five O Clock Club we say, "after the first interview, only 20% of your influencing job is done." The follow-up is another way to distance yourself from the competition.

Let us tell you first what a follow-up note **is not**. By the way at the 5OCC we call them "influencing notes."

- It is not a thank-you note.
- It is not a "what are the next steps" note.
- It is not a "let's keep in touch" note.
- It is not a "I am looking forward to . . ." note.

It is . . . a strong influencing letter or email. From time to time consider, if you have legible handwriting, sending a follow-up via snail mail. Handwritten letters are so seldom seen they often get unusually positive attention.

As you write your influencing letter think about incorporating one or more of the following ideas:

- **Send a proposal to the decision maker.**
   One of the best influencing letters we have seen was from a client who was interviewing for a key job in a company that needed a major turnaround. His influencing letter was a 3-month turnaround plan, complete with early wins, a restructuring proposal and a budget. Yes, he got the job.
- **Personalize your follow-up letters to each person you interviewed with . . . and to the executive assistant who organized the meetings!**
- **The content needs to focus on their key business issues and how you can best influence them.**
- **Outline your fit in their culture.**

Remember there are two main thought processes in every selection process. Can the candidate do the job and do we think he or she will fit into our culture?

What Are Your Resources For Building a Powerful Influencing Letter?

Your interview notes. Many people are not comfortable taking notes but we strongly recommend them. We don't recommend copious notes. They should be brief but legible and you need to immediately expand upon them as soon as you are out of the building. If you don't, key details will be lost. As someone observed, "*the ink from mental notes evaporates quickly.*"

Debrief each interview separately and consider the following:

- What was the tone of each conversation?
- What were the business issues each person was most concerned about?
- What were the positives about you?

- What were some possible objections?
- What could you do to get an early win? Could you send them an idea that might help them with their challenge(s)? Could you send an appropriate article or source?
- Were you able to build rapport around any common interest or hobbies?
- What was the general atmosphere like?
- How was your rapport with the executive assistant?
- How was your rapport with HR?
- Do you know anything about your competition? Can you bolster your case without criticizing them?

Before You Say Yes To A job Offer . . . Check Out the New Boss and the New Culture.

"How do you feel about working for a boss who takes his frustrations out on his employees on a regular basis?"

Over the last two years we have noticed an alarming theme in the stories about how our clients jobs ended—or were about to end. **About sixty percent** have told us, *had they known more* about their future bosses and the corporate culture, they would have *never* accepted their last job.

We began to ask ourselves, what was missing in their process? Well, we found some **serious gaps in their due diligence**. So we developed some questions to improve their due diligence:

- How much time did you actually spend with your future boss? (Two hours is *not* a good answer.)
- Did you spend any time with your boss's boss?
- Did you meet with all of your peers?
- Did you interview or meet with your potential subordinates?
- Did you speak with the key players *outside* your area, people who would be critical to your success?
- Did you talk to anyone who *used to* work for the company?
- Did you talk to anyone who had worked for your future boss within the last few years?
- If the position involves sales or marketing, did you talk to any customers?
- How well did you check out the company financially?
- Is the company vulnerable to be acquired? Or more directly, is it being shopped?
- Are their any blogs dealing with this company or the industry? If yes, have you checked the blog for rumors of reorganizations, or any data that might give you pause?
- If there is a founder? Did you get to meet him or her?
- Was there anyone on the interview list that you didn't get to meet?

The answers to these questions from the *sixty-percent (unhappy) crowd* were unsettling.

- The average time spent in the interview process with the potential new boss was less than three hours and most had not spent any quality time with the boss's boss.
- Few had met more than one or two peers.
- Few had talked to their potential subordinates.
- Almost no one had talked to anyone outside their functional area.

- No one had reached out to former employees of the company.
- Nobody had talked to customers.

Here are the three key reasons jobs deteriorate to the point of resignation or termination:

1. **Number one issue: The Boss**. The bosses turned out to have some serious shortcomings. Comments about **The Boss** included: "world class micro-manager," "abusive," "substance-abuse problem," "only focused on what went wrong," "never complimented the staff even when things were going well," "not a coach or mentor," "loved to take all the credit." Or the boss resigned or moved to another area of the company less than 60 days after the executive came on board.
2. The business was not as financially healthy as portrayed.
3. There was no team culture but a lot of rhetoric masking ego-driven politics and a silo culture.

OK, so what can you do to find out what you are getting into?

At the Five O'Clock Club we stress the importance of the 'consultant mentality' which means finding out as much as you can about the company and the culture *before* you join them. Consultants are expected to probe. They're *paid* to probe. Of course no one is paying you to interview like a consultant. The payoff will come if you really understand what saying 'yes' will get you into!

How much should you probe? One side of our brain says but if I probe maybe they will think I am too aggressive. The key is to manage your anxiety.

For a moment think about the last time you hired someone to build a deck or remodel a kitchen. We bet you were incredibly thorough.

- You took a serious amount of time to check out the contractor(s).
- You went through the project in agonizing detail to make sure the builder understood *exactly* what you wanted.
- You checked multiple references.
- You dropped by to see one or two of the kitchens or decks the builder completed.

Bottom line, you acted like a consultant. We would also bet serious money you were more methodical and cautious about hiring the contractor than you were about analyzing the last few jobs you've said 'yes' to.

So please remember your remodeled kitchen or new deck the next time you are coming down to the wire considering a job offer.

Here are some tips:

- Get a grasp of your potential new boss's management style. Not that you can change it, but it is a great way to size up your chances of living with the quirks.
- Find out about the corporate culture especially how decisions are made.
- Will you be able to address performance issues quickly, and have final say about hiring and firing?
- How will your future peers view your arrival? Will *they* agree or support the key goals you've been asked to achieve?
- Who, outside your department, is critical to your success; are *they* committed to help you succeed? Have you talked to them?
- How is your function perceived and why?
- How do key customers perceive the company?

This is a lot to find out. But you need a 'consultant mentality,' and this means *being curious* and trying to locate the minefields.

We have found that managers and executives who make hiring decisions are impressed with candidates who have done their homework and **ask tough but fair questions**. This is not a time to be shy or cautious. You don't want to look back and say to yourself, "why didn't I ask more questions?"

Key Assumptions for Due Diligence:

- All of the points we have made are only appropriate when a company has shown genuine interest in your candidacy.
- This level of inquiry is recommended **after the first round of interviews**. We believe it is inappropriate in the early stages of the interview process.

Here are some of the tough-but-fair questions you need to ask:

- "If I were to interview your staff, what are they going to say about what it's like working for you? What do they like about your management style? What will *they* say drives them crazy?

  TIP: Always ask these questions with a smile.

- "What is your process for keeping your team informed? How often do you communicate to the team as a group? When was the last time you communicated to the group? What was the agenda?"

- "How will you measure my success? What will be the metrics? What will constitute outstanding performance in the first 6 months? The first year?"

Notice if the manager can describe success in quantifiable outcomes. If he can't in the interview, he probably can't when you are working for him either.

- Who has the boss or manager successfully mentored and how?
- Here's a really tough one: ask to see the boss's résumé. Seeing the résumé will help you understand his or her track record. If you don't feel comfortable asking for the résumé, you can at least ask, "Do you have a bio that I can review?"
- Check references! Obviously, most of us wince at the very thought of asking a future boss for references. You need to talk to several people who have worked for this person. In fact, we have a client who was interviewing with a CEO and the CEO suggested our client talk to some people who had worked for him. His comment was, "John, this is an important career move for you. You need to understand what it is like to work for me and there is no better way than to talk to some people who have."

    TIP: While this maybe obvious, the references cannot be current direct reports. The political currents are just too strong!

Some additional tips:

- Find out what the turnover is by area, especially in sales, leadership positions, and IT.
- Check if there is a blog on the company. There are often real pearls in blogs. The easiest way to do this is type the company name and the word 'blog' into Google or your favorite search engine.
- Talk to your potential peers and ask:
    ✓ "What are the boss's strengths and weaknesses?"
    ✓ "How do you deal with his or her quirks?"
    ✓ "How does the team deal with crisis or short-term performance failures?"
    ✓ "What do you see as the top three priorities for the person being hired?"
    ✓ "What do you see as the company's biggest challenges?"
- Interview the boss's boss. Having heard a few too many horror stories, this is a *must*. We understand that this is not always possible but do everything you

can to make it happen. One of the best ways to make sure everyone is on the same page is to ask the boss's boss many of the same questions.

- Suggested questions for the boss's boss:
  - ✓ What are the company's top two or three priorities?
  - ✓ What do you see as your major challenges and priorities?
  - ✓ What will constitute outstanding performance in my first six months?
  - ✓ What are the key issues in the first year? And again, how will my performance be measured?
- Interview your key internal customers. A few examples:
  - ✓ If you are in marketing, interview some folks on the sales team.
  - ✓ If you are in sales, interview some folks in marketing.
  - ✓ If your role is in HR or Finance, meet with the heads of the key functions you would support.
- Interview several major customers of the company. This can be invaluable on two fronts. First it gives you some real world business perspectives, and second, if you accept the position, you have already begun to build important relationships.

Interview as a consultant and ask all the right people all the right questions. This will put you head and shoulders above your competition. Very few candidates are this thorough, and high-performing organizations truly appreciate potential employees who know what it means to do due diligence.

Chapter Summary ....

- **Direct Contact including Direct and Targeted Mailings. Both** are important tactics for your job search. Remember our study showed that our executive clients got 30% of their first meetings by contacting directly people they had never met and **had not been referred in to**. And over **20% of all jobs are found through direct-mail campaigns**
- **Executive Recruiters**. When they call with a job that is at the right level but not at the right company consider exploring it. It is good practice, it is a chance to develop a relationship with the recruiter, and you may, be pleasantly surprised about the opportunity once you get more details.
- **Navigating Internet Ads.** A major time-saver is using a good job aggregator such as Indeed.com. Stay on top of the current best job aggregators. Use

Google or the equivalent. Just type in: "best executive job aggregators" and you will instantly have the latest.

- **The keys to successful interviewing.** Please re-read this section before every interview.
- One more time: **Interview like a consultant** and ask all the right people all the right questions.
- **Due diligence**. This is an absolute must. If you were to do only one piece of due diligence we recommend doing thorough reference checks on your potential boss. This means talking to people who used to work for him or her and who will be candid about strengths and weaknesses. Our experience shows good leaders have no problem giving you lots of references but if you get that "deer in the headlights look" when you ask, your suspicions will have been confirmed!

8
...

Campaign Management:
Running A Successful Search

Chapter Overview ....

- Managing the momentum of your search
- Key metrics for assessing a successful search

....

Managing Your Momentum

We have a great model for helping you do this. You will view your search from the perspective of just three phases. Like any good project management process it lets you stay on top of all the details. You will also see it pulls together everything we have discussed in the first seven chapters, so it is a good refresher.

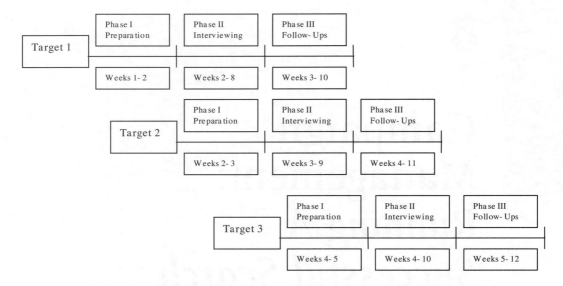

Phase 1. Preparation

The preparation phase is all about . . . preparation.

- You have completed your research which allowed you to identify all the companies in your target market within your targeted geographic preferences.

For example if one of your target market was investment banks in the NY Metropolitan area, you now have a list of all the banks by name. (Chapter 4)

- You have developed a hard hitting résumé and cover letters. (Chapter 5)
- You have crafted a compelling Two-Minute Pitch. (Chapter 4)
- You have developed a marketing plan that includes the names of your target companies. (Chapter 3)
- Now it is time to begin lining up interviews, and lining up interviews is all about persistence and numbers.

Whether you are using networking or direct contact to get to the decision maker, your primary objective is to get in front of decision makers at the right level in the right companies. It is not important that there is an opening. In fact, although it sounds a bit counter-intuitive, you are more likely to get better market and networking information when there isn't a job at stake. You will be more relaxed and so will they.

Setting up the interviews is going to take persistence. In the world of selling we know it takes 8–10 calls before you can get to a decision maker. The data is no different

"I don't need to interview you. I can get all the info I need from the 12,761 e-mails you sent me."

in the world of job hunting. Five O'Clock Club data shows it takes, on average, 8 calls to schedule a face-to-face meeting.

It is also a numbers game. We thought the best way to demonstrate this was with a case study based upon one of our client's experiences. Fortunately Adam keep very good records and his numbers are fairly typical of what it takes to complete a successful search on a timely basis.

Adam's target position was the Director of the Exotic Derivatives Desk (EDD) at an investment bank in the New York metro area. First he researched all the investment banks that currently had or were planning to have one or more EDD's. He uncovered 105. He then called every single one. You will notice the number of decision makers is larger than the number of companies and that is because in several banks there were multiple decision makers. It was just four months from the time Adam uncovered the 105 targets until he got his first offer.

Total companies contacted	Numer of deci- sions makers contacted	Average number of calls per decision maker	Number of interviews where there was no opening	Number of interviews for open positions	Number of offers
105	155	6	30	6	3

Phase 2. Interviewing

So now you are getting in front of decision makers! Here are the key things to focus on:

- Prepare for your interviews with a "consultant's mindset." (Chapter 7) Research and strategize just like a consultant pitching a proposal to a prospective client or pitching your boss on why they should give you more headcount.
- Get as much information from each interview as you are giving.
- Learn the business issues important to each person in the interview process.
- Ask what they think your strengths are for the position?
- Ask where they are in the hiring process?
- Ask how you compare with the other candidates?
- Ask if they have any reservations about hiring you?
- Think about the best strategies for overcoming any of their objections.
- Clarify the next steps in the process.

Phase 3. Follow-up

A strong follow-up letter is one of the best ways to distance yourself from your competition. So we are going to review the most important elements of good follow-up letter as well as some of those creative touches we have seen others use successfully. You will notice in The Five O'Clock Club methodology we never use the words "thank-you notes." This is because your follow-up communications need to be influencing letters not thank-you notes. You also need to do this after every interview, not just the first.

- A friendly reminder: the best preparation for writing a strong follow-up letter is taking good notes in every meeting.

  TIP: If you are not comfortable taking detailed notes, take enough notes so when you debrief the interviews you will remember most of the details. And do your debrief ASAP or we guarantee the details will evaporate.

- Write a personalized letter (email or snail-mail) to each person you interviewed. Before writing the letters please ask yourself (as we suggested in the last chapter) the following:
  ✓ What was the tone of the conversation? Friendly? Formal? Was the person a schmoozer or bottom line? Learn anything personal, like a hobby? Your follow-up letter should mirror the tone of the meeting. Take their style into consideration. If they were folksy then a folksy letter would be fine. If they were fairly bottom-line then you want your follow-up to be to the point.
  ✓ Did anything come up that would make them want you to be part of their team?
  ✓ What did they like about you and your experience? Be sure to reinforce those points.
  ✓ Any objections? Best to hit these head on without being defensive.
  ✓ What were the key business issues from each person's perspective? When all is said and done, most important is their perception of your value around solving those issues. A good technique is to simply summarize your understanding of the challenges and how you could add value.
  ✓ Don't be afraid to share your passion around an issue(s).
- Creative touches with follow-up letters we have seen:
  ✓ The company was doing their first international product launch that had some unique cultural nuances to it. The candidate developed a suggested approach to deal with the cultural nuances and included those in her follow-up letter.
  ✓ The company was about to have a national sales meeting without a SVP of Sales and even though the candidate was interviewing for the job the hiring process would not be completed in time. He sent a proposal along with his follow-up letter that outlined how they could pull it off without negatively impacting the sales force.
  ✓ A candidate for the VP of Marketing included a PowerPoint presentation comparing the company's top three products against their key competitor's products.

The Three Stages . . . The Key Metrics For Measuring The Success Of Your Search.

How soon can I begin measuring how I am doing?

You can start measuring the progress of your search **as soon as you have developed a list of your targeted companies**.

To do this, The Five O'Clock Club process divides the search into three stages. Stage-1 contacts, Stage-2 contacts and Stage-3 contacts. Your three stages become your "sales pipeline" and you become both the sales manager and the sales rep. As the sales manager you'll review your sales rep's results every week. As the sales rep, you will focus on having the best possible pipe line you can. As everyone knows, in the real world it takes a great pipeline to get great sales. In the job search world having a great "job pipeline" works. In this case the great sale means landing the right job.

Stage-1 Contacts

Stage 1 is the foundation of your pipeline. At the beginning of your search it will contain the names of people you know but as your search progresses it will also contain lots of people you don't currently know. You need a minimum of 6–10 people in Stage 1 from day one. Some of our clients have gotten the numbers to over 100 contacts after a few months. We know this looks like a big number but don't get discouraged. One of our clients started with just 10 in her first month but got up to 350 by the end of the second month.

At the start of your search the qualities of your Stage-1 contacts should look like this:

- Your closest business associates who you are regularly in touch with.
- Anyone you know who knows something about your target market(s) and your target companies.
- Senior managers and executives who know you and are in a position to hire you or recommend you be hired.
- Everyone in your personal network who cares about you and wants to help.

Guidelines for organizing and staying in touch with your Stage-1 contacts:

- Put everyone's name in your Contact Manager with all the appropriate information including when you talked to them last and what you talked about.
- Plan to follow-up at lease once a month with everyone who has been helpful. The follow-up should include giving them progress reports of how you

are doing, how a contact they gave you was helpful or sharing with them the names of new targets you have added in case they know something about the new targets.

- Stage-1 contacts who have not been helpful should be removed from your database.

TIPS:

1. Not staying in touch with Stage-1 contacts is the single biggest cause of networks drying up.
2. In addition to keeping everyone aware of your targeted companies also share with them the names of executives and experts you have come across in your research. This takes advantage of the "it's a small world" phenomena we have all experienced.

Stage-2 Contacts

Stage-2 contacts are executives who are at the *right level*, in the *right positions*, and in the *right companies* in your target market. They are the decision makers or the influencers. Remember the influencers are the folks the decision makers listen to. They are the ones who may get you hired when a position opens up. When meeting with influences, you should hear things like, "I wish we had an opening, you would be perfect," or "there are some things in the works that we would like to talk to you about very soon," or "if you don't hear from us in two weeks, please call me." By the way, if your Stage-2 contacts are not saying these kinds of things you need to find out why. Sometimes you just have to take the lead and ask, "if you had an opening, would you hire someone like me?"

So how many Stage-2 contacts do you need? The magic numbers are still 6–10 if you want to complete a timely search.

Guidelines for organizing and staying in touch with your Stage-2 contacts:

- Good follow-up is always a critical tactic but in Stage 2 not following up could mean losing out on a great job.
- Keep your name in front of them at least every three to four weeks. One way to do that, without being perceived as a pest, is to send "gifts." The gift can be an email with a timely business article attached or an article related to their personal interests or hobby.
- Again, put everyone's name in your Contact Manager and note whether each is an influencer or a decision maker.

Stage-3 Contacts

Stage-3 contacts are executives who are at the *right level*, in the *right positions*, in the *right companies* who have a current opening or who are considering creating an opening that fits your criteria. And yes, you need to have 6–10 opportunities in this stage too. There are three primary reasons: first, four or five things can fall off the plate at any one time through no fault of your own; second, you need the critical mass that will produce two or three offers; and last, without 6–10 your search will take a lot longer.

In Stage 3 you are now in the running so your focus needs to be 110% on maintaining your momentum. This can be more challenging than it sounds. It is not unusual for a candidate to be brought back three or four times and for the process to take months to complete. This trend started in the 1990's and it happened for a couple of reasons. One reason was the "dot com" meltdown where many companies got burned by hiring fast but not smart. The other reason is the fact that turnover is both costly and disruptive, so companies have become more cautious.

Stage-3 Follow-up TIPS:

- Review the guidelines in the beginning of this chapter regarding the keys to good follow-up.
- Do not be afraid to use your key contacts who also know the decision makers and influencers. If they are well respected by the decision makers you need their endorsement. The quickest way is have them call or email the decision maker. The message should be short, to the point and contain a performance example. It might sound like this, "John, I understand you are considering Sue Mason for your VP Product Development. I just wanted you to know that when we worked together she was a star. She turned around the entire department in less than six months."

Case Study: How Rebecca Went From Stage 1 to Stage 3 in Less Than 4 Weeks

We want to introduce you to one of our clients, Rebecca Adams. When we met Rebecca she was a successful strategy consultant in one of the top 10 global consulting firms. She wanted to transition to the client side and one of her targets was ABC, Inc., a $100M packaged goods company. The position was Senior Director of Strategy. The decision maker she was targeting was Patrick, the CEO. At the time she thought of approaching ABC, Rebecca did not know if there was an open position.

Where Did Rebecca Find Her Stage-1 Contacts?

Rebecca first checked to see if she knew anybody who worked at ABC, or anybody who was close to ABC as a client, a supplier, or a partner.

Here are Rebecca's Stage-1 contacts for ABC:

- Bob, chairman of a professional association with connections to several consultants who work with ABC.
- Chris, a former colleague who made a similar transition.
- Leesa, an alum from grad school, who was the CMO at one of ABC's key suppliers.
- Eckart, a former direct report, currently a marketing manager at ABC.

How did Rebecca Develop Stage-2 Contacts from Stage-1 Contacts?

Bob, chairman of the professional association, introduced her to a consultant who worked closely with Patrick, the CEO of ABC. The consultant could not introduce her to Patrick, but gave her a valuable piece of information: ABC is strongly considering opening a position in strategic planning at her level.

Chris and Leesa introduced Rebecca to two potentially strong Stage-2 contacts, Meegan, the CFO and Mark, the SVP of Operations.

Eckart, Rebecca's former direct report introduced her to his boss Donald, the VP of Marketing at ABC. Eckart was not sure if Donald would be the decision maker, but he was a strong influencer.

How Rebecca got to Patrick, her Stage-3 Contact.

Rebecca started calling Meegan and Mark, her two new Stage-2 contacts. Unfortunately she did not reach them despite several follow up calls. She then called Donald in hope of getting his help to gain access to Meegan or Mark. In fact, he agreed to meet with her for an informal discussion and was impressed. At the end of the meeting, he called Patrick's (the CEO's) assistant and set up a meeting for her. Rebecca just got her Stage-3 meeting.

As you can see not all Stage-1 Contacts gave Rebecca valuable Stage-2 contacts. Logic would tell us Meegan and Mark would be her best bets when, in fact, it was Eckart, her former direct report, and Donald, his boss, who led her to the job!

The lesson here is that "old saw," persistence. Rebecca did a wonderful job of "leaving no contact un-called" and it paid off.

Summary: How it all fits together:

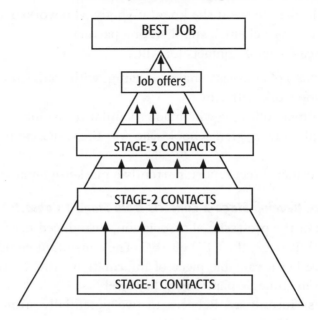

Chapter Summary ....

- **A strong follow-up letter** is one of the best ways to distance yourself from your competitors. It needs to be personalized and we recommend you don't copy anyone. Trust they will share the letters.
- Personalized means focusing on that person's issues and whenever possible mentioning how you could add value to solving those issues.
- Don't be afraid to be creative. Could you do a high impact PowerPoint presentation, a competitive analysis or write a business proposal?
- Pay attention to Stages 1, 2, and 3. Just like everywhere in the world of business it is all about the numbers. Remember The Five O'Clock Club mantra: "6 to 10 things in the works," at every stage. As one of our clients said, "hey, this is more work than work!"

9
...

Getting and Staying Organized:
Critical To A Timely, Successful Search

Chapter Overview

- Tips for setting up a home office
- Tips to micro-manage your search
- The do's and don'ts of time management

Executive Summary

- **Home office.** Most of you will choose to conduct your job search from a home office. We recommend it be solely dedicated to your job search, complete with a private phone line, filing system, computer, internet access and business e-mail address. If not, inevitably, your personal and family stuff will find its way into the middle of important search materials. Not a good thing.

- **Managing the details.** Using **Contact Manager Software (CMS) is a must.** It is the only way to stay on top of the all the gory details involved in managing your search. With CMS at your finger tips you will never be caught off guard (read: no brain freezes) when one of your contacts, a prospective employer or a key executive recruiter calls you back unexpectedly. And CMS will make follow-up absolutely painless.
- **Time Management.** In this crazy 24/7 world everyone is time challenged so we provide a quick refresher on what to do and not to do later in this chapter.

Your Office

This is the first step to getting organized: set up a **fully dedicated** job-search office. Our clients do one of the following:

- ✓ Most set up a home office.
- ✓ Some rent outside space, especially when total privacy is impossible at home. They usually find space through their network, like a family attorney or accountant, that is available on a month-to-month basis.
- ✓ Some use the "condo" offices now available in most cities. A condo office allows you to rent by the hour, week or month. They are private offices, fully furnished including phone, voice mail, and a personal computer (usually with DSL or T1 access), plus copying and fax support.

TIPS For Setting Up a Home Office

- A dedicated desk and filing system. We say "dedicated" because clients who have a desk full of family and personal materials or share the desk with other family members have consistently been the ones who seem to lose important networking and contact information. They are the ones asking us, "how can I stay better organized?"
- Order a dedicated phone line with phone company voice mail (VM), not an answering machine. Phone company VM picks up any time you are on the line. Connecting with you by phone will be the first impression so it is important it mirrors a professional office.

Your VM message should be just like the one you had when employed. Please make sure it is upbeat and there is energy and a smile in your voice.

TIP: No call waiting on this phone. Putting someone on hold is never cool and it is incredibly annoying to the person who is calling you.

- Have your computer on a dedicated line, DSL preferable. You need to be able to talk on the phone and view the computer at the same time. This is particularly important when the caller (or you) wants to review a shared document.
- Set up a separate email address. If possible, use your name, for example PeteSmith@whatever.com. This may seem like a minor point but it allows people to easily see and remember your name. We suggest using the name you go by at work so if it is Pete vs. Peter then use Pete in the email address. Please avoid the temptation to be clever, like golfaddict@pinehurst.com. Only your golf buddies will be impressed.

What If Managing the Detail Is a Pain?

We wish there were a good answer for this. Managing the details is a pain but like most important tasks "the devil is in the details!"

Some clients actually hire a virtual assistant. Frequently it is someone who has worked for them in the past and is interested in working some evenings or weekends for extra income. Most, however, decide it is better to handle the details themselves.

Managing the Detail

A quick quiz about the detail you need to stay on top of:

- Can you easily access info on everyone you have met?
- Have you captured what you have told them about your search?
- Have you captured important information about them?
- Do you know who referred you to whom and why?
- Do you have a foolproof method for reminding yourself when you need to call them back or follow-up?

If you are having challenges answering yes to any of these questions you are likely to have a few embarrassing moments during your search. Worse you may even loose out on some important opportunities.

Fortunately there are some easy solutions but first we want to share with you one of those embarrassing calls from one of our "not so organized" clients, and then a successful call.

Here is the call from Mary Smith to John.

Situation: It is January and John is 2 months into his search. The good news is John is a natural networker and has already talked to over 250 people since he started. He has over a dozen Stage-2 contacts. Unfortunately John has not put the same energy into managing his contacts as he did in developing them.

His office, to put it kindly, is a bit disorganized. He is now trying to write several important follow up notes and three influencing letters. Papers are spread out all over his desk. His children just got back from school and are blowing off "after school energy" at what seems to be 130 decibels. The phone rings and it is Mary Smith, a senior HR manager. John does not use a contact manager but keeps his contacts in a stack of Manila folders and on some 3x5 cards.

Let's listen in on the call. (Fortunately he did quiet down his kids before picking up the phone.)

Mary: Hi John. It's Mary Smith.

John: Oh Hi Mary (John is madly thinking to himself, who is Mary Smith?)

Mary: I am happy to get a hold of you. I've been meaning to return your call for a while.

John: (Frantically shuffling papers) Oh great! Thanks! (Again, madly thinking, what call? When?).

Mary: (She can hear the shuffling of papers but is too polite to say anything.) I have good news. I've just talked to Eddie.

John: Oh (long pause) great! (Eddie, who is Eddie?)

Needless to say this call was a disaster and John quickly became a non-candidate. Here is the call to an organized candidate.

Situation: Janet has a similar situation with kids coming home from school and all the usual distractions but in this case Janet is using **Contact Manager Software(CMS)**. Janet planned, early in her search, how she was going to stay on top of all the details. One of the disciplines she developed was to enter information into her Contact Manager every time she met someone or someone contacted her.

Here is how the call went for Janet.

Mary: Hi Janet. It's Mary Smith.

Janet: (Immediately accessed Mary's record from her CMS and scanned her notes.) Hi Mary, nice to hear back from you. How was your vacation in the Caribbean? (Another detail she captured and entered into her CMS.)

Mary: Great, thank you, nice of you to ask. Listen, I have good news. I just talked to Eddie.

Janet: (Quickly accessing the file where she has stored information about Eddie). It's interesting you mention Eddie. I just read his interview with the *Financial Times* two days ago. Sounds like you guys are getting some great coverage on your latest security product.

Mary: Yes we are, in fact that's why I'm calling. We have just posted the Director of Marketing position for this product line and would like you to interview.

CMS is a must for keeping you on top of your game.

There are dozens of good CMS programs out there, many for under $100. However we find most of our clients already own Microsoft Outlook 2003 which is a very effective contact manager. We don't have a favorite to recommend but we do want to highlight **what any good CMS can do for you**:

- Provide you with an electronic address book that is instantly accessible from your desk top, lap top or PDA.
- Allows you to capture the names, addresses and contact information for everyone you meet.
- Include a note-taking capability so you can record the key points of any conversation, or whether the contact is a Yankee fan, collects antiques or enjoys the opera.
- Allows you to send emails to groups of people. The groups can be organized any way that makes sense to you.
- Record whether they are a Stage 1, 2 or 3 contact.
- Automatically reminds you to call back on a set dates **making follow-up painless**.
- Automatically notify you of birthdays and anniversaries.
- Allows you to review all previous emails sent to the contact and the person's replies.
- Eliminates the need for spreadsheets or a gazillion manila folders.

Had poor John had a contact manager he too may have landed an interview for the Director of Marketing position.

Time management Do's and just a few Don'ts

These are very fundamental but like the fundamentals in your favorite sport or hobby if they aren't practiced regularly your game suffers.

Do . . .

- Begin everyday with a written "to do" list. Written goals get completed on a much more timely basis than the unwritten. Remember, the ink on those mental notes evaporates almost instantly.
- Set achievable goals. A written "to do" list is a must but not if it has 15 priorities on it.
- Use your daytime hours for network calls, direct-contact calls and follow-up calls.
- Work in an area with minimum distractions.
- Take short breaks every hour, just five to ten minutes. You will stay more energized and get less frustrated.
- Exercise regularly, even if it is just a walk around the block. In fact the famous Cooper Clinic (the original aerobics guys) found, in their most recent research on cardio-fitness, we need only 20 minutes just three times a week to maintain it. Exercise, as all of you know, is a proven stress reliever. And there is definitely stress during a job search.
- Watch the alcohol consumption. Remember it is a depressant and makes many of us more fatigued the next day.
- Get adequate rest. You no longer have to worry about being in the office by 7:30AM.
- You know the drill about eating well which includes snacking well. Lot's of carrot sticks and celery rather than chips. Studies show eating well also keeps us more alert.
- **Keep repeating the time management mantra** . . . is what I am doing, right now, the best thing I can be doing to move my job campaign forward?
- Celebrate your successes no matter how small. Brag to the family and buddies when you have had a productive day or connected with someone important.
- Use the weekend or evenings for straightening up the office.

Don't . . .

- Use daytime hours for surfing the web for jobs. This is critical networking time.
- Watch TV, play video games or mow the lawn during business hours.

Some Time Management Tips When Doing Research.

One of the more time consuming steps of the search process is doing the research on your target companies and your target markets. Here are some tips on how to make it less time consuming:

✓ Always start your research with a plan even if is just a few notes or questions to yourself. EGS: What is the key data I am looking for and why? Will knowing this data help me in the interview? Will this data let me better evaluate this company as a viable target?

✓ Avoid getting mesmerized with your internet searches. They can eat up hours of valuable time. Also this can be avoided if you follow the first tip, starting with a plan.

✓ Set aside a certain amount of time per target. Challenge yourself to see how much information you can find on one target in 15 minutes or less. This will actually become fun and you will amaze yourself at some of your results. Note: this time target does not include printing out information.and reading it, just finding it.

✓ Consider doing some of your research at the library where you won't be distracted by phone calls, email or other interruptions.

Chapter Summary

- Staying on top of your search details will not only help you conduct a more effective search but knowing you are on top of the details will greatly reduce your anxiety and increase your confidence.
- Please remember, **untimely follow-up** is one of the biggest momentum killers.
- **Using Contact Manager Software will go a long way to keeping you on top of both!**

10
····

The Two Big S's:
Salary and Severance

Chapter Overview ....

- A quick review of the principles of negotiation
- Importance of having a negotiating team
- The Five O'Clock Club's Four Step salary negotiation process
- Tips on creative negotiating
- Tips for reference checks

Principles of Negotiation

- It has to be win-win. Motherhood? Yes, but a critical mindset. It helps to write down the areas where you want to stand firm and those you are willing to be more flexible about. Please don't try to wing it.

    TIP: Always begin the negotiating process by reiterating **first what you like about the people** and the opportunity, **then what you like about the offer**. For those rare times where there is nothing to like, tell them you are pleased to have received a formal offer.

- Be non-confrontational. Not that any of our readers would ever fall into category, but it does happen especially when an employment attorney is brought in. It also can happen to you, from the offering side, when they have misunderstood your current comp package. It often sounds like: "we had no idea your bonus was at this level," or "we totally misunderstood your base."

TIPS: If you use an employment attorney make sure you are totally comfortable with his or her style. Make sure the hiring manager understands your current compensation package. **Please do not count on HR or the employment application to do this for you.**

- The last key principle: The first person to mention a number loses. Never tell them what you are "looking for." If they continue to press, just keep telling them your current total compensation and that your only expectations are that they will be fair and market-competitive.

Your Negotiating Team

There are three members you should seriously consider having on your negotiating team:

1. A Five O'Clock Club executive coach who is experienced in salary negotiations. A coach can be an effective sounding board and, just as important, someone you can practice your negotiating points with before you go live.
2. An employment attorney. They can be indispensable as contracts, compensation and benefits packages are getting increasingly complex and global. If your offer is from an organization outside the US make sure your employment attorney is knowledgeable on the international front or is connected to someone who is.
3. Your "advisory board." They know what is going on in your industry, and some members may have recently changed jobs themselves. They will have a solid network that you can tap into in order to effectively evaluate and negotiate the offer.

The Five O'Clock Club Four-Step Salary Negotiation Process

1. **Negotiate the Job.**
Before you consider or respond to any offer, verbal or otherwise, make sure the job

is at the right level, with the right responsibilities, and the right deliverables. If it is not then the offer is likely to be less than you deserve because these are the most critical criteria in determining a job's worth.

The process for doing this begins at the first interview and every subsequent interview. Here are some guidelines to follow:

- ✦ You need everyone's input: boss, the boss's boss, peers and subordinates.
- ✦ Get them all talking about **deliverables** not responsibilities. **The magnitude of the deliverables** will be the primary driver in determining the job's worth. Ask everyone you interview with what they see as the top three deliverables for the job.
- ✦ After meeting with everyone write up what you have heard and bounce it off your **negotiating team**. Ask them, "given these deliverables, what would this job be worth in your company?"
- ✦ At the same time keep playing back to the hiring manager what you have heard from everyone. It might sound like this: "We talked about the key deliverables A & B but I have heard from several of the team members we also need to deliver on C & D, which makes this job's risks and impact significantly larger."

If the job is too light, tell the hiring manager and be prepared to say what could be added to make it appropriate for you. If it sounds heavier than the targeted compensation let them know, as discussed above. Another example of how to cover this: "This sounds like a terrific opportunity and a chance to make a major impact but honestly the job everyone is describing is a notch or two above the compensation you are proposing." Then be prepared for the "why do you think so?" question. One answer could be, you have checked with a number of industry executives who told you they would be paying significantly (be as specific as possible here, for example, 15–20%) more for these deliverables at their companies.

2. Outshine and Outlast Your Competition.

The reality is you will be up against some tough competition but there are some proven techniques that can really separate you from the pack.

- ✦ **Out-listen** your competitors. One more time, our approach is bringing a **consultant's mentality** to every meeting. This means asking the best questions. Where do some of the best questions come from? Your research on the company. Here are a few examples: Why are selling expenses trending up or down? Why have margins been improving or deteriorating? What are the key issues in your business? What are the key drivers of your business? What keeps you up at night? What competitors do you watch the closest? What are the top two or three upside opportunities?

+ **Out-respond** your competitors. One of the best ways to do this is by telling great stories. So instead of answering a question with a "what I would do," tell a story about what you actually did in a similar situation and back it up with data whenever possible.

  You can **out-respond** by writing great influencing letters after every interview that incorporates the business issues discussed. This is where both good note taking and a thorough debriefing of the interview really pay off.

TIP: Debrief as soon as possible with your coach and advisory board.

+ **Out think** your competitors. Do as much due diligence on the company's competitors as possible, especially the competitor's financials. It can give you some killer questions to ask, "Why do your key competitors have a significantly lower cost of sales?" Or when the data is positive, "It is good to see you are doing a great job managing cost of sales."

It may be hard for you to believe but the majority of candidates do not go this extra mile. A good reality test is to think about the last few senior-level candidates you have interviewed. How impressed were you with their preparation? And if you *were* impressed, make sure you are doing the same kinds of things!

3. Get the Offer.

Serious negotiations do not start until you have received a written offer. Some recommended approaches to dealing with a verbal offer:

+ Resist responding to a verbal offer **unless** it exceeds your expectations. We realize this is easy to say but hard to do. Think about what they trying to do with a verbal offer: Get you to commit!

+ If it is a great offer say: "Sounds great and I am flattered but would appreciate a written offer outlining the bonus structure and other details before I formally accept."

+ If it is a terrible offer: "I really like the team, the company and the challenges but honestly your offer doesn't match the deliverables or the responsibilities."

✦ An OK offer: "I am flattered. I can see how I can make a major contribution. If you don't mind I would like to see a written offer that outlines the bonus structure before I formally accept."

4. **Negotiate**

"Since I plan on working for your company for the next 20 years, I was hoping to get all my paychecks up front."

What is negotiable? Everything!

One of the most critical elements to effective negotiating is knowing your market value irrespective of your current or former compensation. The market is the ultimate arbiter.

What is your market value? It is the typical total-compensation package that is offered at your level in your industry and in your geographic area for the particular position you are targeting.

How can you find information about your market value?

- Check salary.com
- Recall other recent interviews where you have been made aware of the compensation package.
- Ask your network, especial senior HR executives you know. They frequently have access to national compensation data.
- Ask any compensation specialists you know. They too will have access to national compensation data.
- Ask executive recruiters you respect.
- Check with your Five O'Clock Club Coach, your mentor and your advisory board.

Here are our coaching points, once you have a written offer:

- Don't rush . . . even if this is your first good offer, and even if they are telling you they want you to start "last week."
- Sit down with your coach, your employment attorney and your "advisory board."
- Remember, there is always money left on the table even when they tell you there isn't. Two key items that are often left off in the early negotiations are a written contract or a severance agreement.
- In the final push go for a written contract in lieu of pushing for more cash. Be sure to include change of ownership language and change of responsibility language. Both should trigger you being able to leave with a full package.
- If a contract is out of the question then discuss a severance agreement.

Key elements should be at least six month's salary continuance, your pro-rated bonus, executive outplacement (with the Five O'Clock Club of course), and full benefits, not COBRA. You will, by law, be offered COBRA at the end of the severance agreement. If you relocated then be sure to negotiate relocation back home.

> TIP: **The best way to discuss severance** is to talk about it in terms of a "safety net." The "safety net" should be discussed in the context of how tenuous executive positions are today due to uncontrollable factors not performance. Also certain industry groups have more turmoil than others so be sure to take that into account as you negotiate.

Things that are customarily negotiated:

- Salary. There is always flexibility.
- Timing of first salary review. Negotiate it to be 6 months sooner.
- Title. Make sure the title they are offering matches the titles of your peers.
- Vacation. At the executive level, a minimum of four weeks.
- Sign-on bonus, especially if the base salary isn't market competitive and if you have left money on the table in your last position.
- Prepaid or guaranteed bonus.
- If stock options, a larger grant.
- Any perk you currently enjoy such as:
  - ✓ Unique insurance coverage
  - ✓ Leadership development
  - ✓ Career coach
  - ✓ Memberships
  - ✓ Car or car allowance
  - ✓ Commuting costs

  TIP: Put a dollar value on all perks you are giving up and leverage the value into your base salary or a sign-on bonus.

Allow yourself to be able to say no if your basic requirements are not met. That's why you need six to ten Stage 3's in the works. It is easier to say "no" to the wrong compensation package if you know you are getting close with 2 or 3 other companies.

You will be amazed at the power a true "no" has. If the company knows you are ready to leave the negotiating table, you don't even have to say that you have other offers. And if you are the right candidate, chances are they will move in your direction because no one wants to settle for the number two choice or start the process all over again.

Final Negotiating Questions To Consider

- If the company does an IPO, will I be offered stock?
- If new deferred compensation plans are created, will I be eligible?
- What is the compensation package for the next two levels?
- If I am performing above plan when will I be considered for a promotion?
- Who are the key decision makers for making a promotion happen?
- What has been the merit increase percentage for high performers over the last two years?

Creative Negotiating

A few alternatives to accepting the job:

- Consider becoming a consultant for the company. In some circumstances, it might be a better move to negotiate a consulting contract. A few examples:
  - ✦ You are not sure about the long-term potential of the job.
  - ✦ You are not sure about the stability of the company.
  - ✦ You cannot come to terms on the compensation level.
  - ✦ You are not sure this is the right job for you, but you need the income.
- Negotiate a temporary contract. Here is how one of our CEO clients did this.

Sally was thrilled when she received an offer as the CEO of a gourmet food company. Her base compensation was slightly above market but the bonus structure was considerably below market. She was being asked to tackle a very challenging turnaround with aggressive revenue growth goals but her performance bonus did not give her a fair share of the results.

Sally was convinced she would achieve the results but there was resistance from the Board over changing her performance bonus. So she sat down with her boss and proposed a six-month contract that stayed with the original performance bonus but would give her a sign-on bonus plus add some accelerators for overachievement. Her boss agreed immediately.

Six months later she had exceeded even the best-case performance scenario and ended up re-negotiating her contract with a larger performance bonus than she ever dreamt would be possible.

Reference Checks

Reference checks are key to help you outdistance your competition.

You may think by the offer stage you have eliminated your competition but you know you haven't. Remember what you did the last time you hired for a key position? Chances are you waited until the candidate accepted your offer before turning down the other strong candidates. This means if the reference checks do not go well, they will revert to another candidate.

Take particular care in choosing your references. They can strongly contribute to your getting ahead in this race. Chances are, they will want to talk to at least two bosses, two peers and two subordinates from the recent past. If your references are from more than five years ago that will be a red flag.

Your references need to be well briefed and we strongly suggest you script all of them, not just your former bosses. An effective way to script your references is to send them a document that outlines talking points. Frame the talking points by saying something like, "Linda, if you are comfortable with what I have written, this is what I would appreciate you covering."

Your script should include the questions, based on all your interviews, that are most likely to come up. Be sure to include the tough ones as well as the obvious. One of the most obvious questions for all your former bosses will be, would they hire you again if they could? As obvious as this is, many clients don't cover it.

Chapter Summary

- The number one strategy is to always, always, always *negotiate the job first*. If the job isn't at the right level the compensation won't be either.
- To maximize your compensation potential set up a negotiating team. This team should be made up of your Five O'Clock Club Coach, your employment attorney and your advisory board.

  TIP: Don't over-rely on them. They should only be used for advice and counsel. You should always be in charge.

- That old saw: "everything is negotiable" is true.
- If you are at an impasse consider creative alternatives like Sally did when she negotiated a six-month contract first or a lucrative consulting project.

11

How To Deal With The Emotional Roller-Coaster Of Job Search

Chapter Overview ··

- Dealing with the highs
- Tips for coping with the inevitable lows
- A quick health, fitness and spiritual audit

··

The Emotional Roller Coaster.

The first thing we want to tell you is, it is **absolutely normal** to experience lows during your job search. Looking for a new job has long been recognized as a major life stressor. In fact if you were to tell us you were not feeling any stress we would be really concerned!

Dealing With the Highs.

Managing the highs is almost more important than managing the lows. Why? Because, **well managed highs help us build powerful momentum**. Our definition of a "high" is when you are feeling confident about your search.

Highs can be triggered by the simplest things: a returned call, a receptive executive recruiter, a networking meeting, or someone unexpectedly calling to volunteer some information. It makes us feel great but sometimes we are tempted to sit back, relax and enjoy the feeling. We want you to enjoy the feeling but not to sit back and relax. Use the extra adrenaline to build momentum in your search. Here are a couple of ways to do that:

- Let everyone in your network know how you are doing especially those who have been helpful. **Remember to be specific**: "I just had a great interview with Dana Smith at Citicorp." Why? People will email you back saying, "I don't know Dana but I know an SVP in Operations there." Bingo, you have just expanded your network at one of your target companies. The flip side is someone who lets her network know but in generalities: "I just had a great interview with a major financial services company." She misses a great opportunity to expand her network. No one can add value to this communication other than say something like "that's great."
- Make more networking calls when your confidence is high especially direct contact calls. Your confidence will come through over the phone.
- Do more direct and targeted mailings.
- Add at least 10 new companies to your target list.

Following through on any of these suggestions is going to result in increased confidence, more contacts in Stage 1 and 2, and more momentum!

Dealing With the Lows or "Being Down."

We have found one of the single biggest causes of "lows" has nothing to to do with a serious emotional state. It is because, in over 90% of the cases, the client simply hasn't been executing on the process. Therefore the first thing we ask you to do is a "little operations review" or "audit" with yourself. Candidly go through the following outline and you literally write down your answers.

In General

- Are you spending enough time on your search? We recommend at least 35 hours a week if you are unemployed, 15 hours a week if you are employed.
- Have you grown your Stage-1 contacts well beyond "6–10?"
- What is the status of your "6 to 10 things" in Stages 2 and 3?
- Do you think you spent enough time on the assessment exercises?

- Are you spending enough time researching prior to every interview? "Enough time" means your research giving you information that is impressing whomever you are talking to.
- Are you using Contact Manager Software to keep you organized and on top of your follow-ups?

Assessment

- Have you been too quick in selecting your targets?
- Do you have critical mass? You will need to target at least 200 positions to complete your search in a reasonable amount of time which means closer to six months than 12 months.
- Are your targets specific enough? Once you have chosen an industry you then need to have the names of specific companies.
- Have you ranked your targets so you are working on your top priorities?

Preparation Phase

- Are you relying on only one technique to get interviews? Two of the most common traps are either focusing only on networking or only looking for openings (online or print).

For your search to be effective you need to be doing it all:

Direct contact (remember 30% of our surveyed executives got their first interview this way), networking, retained search executives, print and online ads (including those on the company website), as well as targeted and direct mail campaigns.

- Are you contacting the right people at the right level in your targeted companies?
- Have you checked how your pitch, résumé and cover letters position you? The best way to get feedback here is to ask "**how does my résumé, pitch or cover letter position me?**" not, "what do you think about my résumé or cover letter." Who you ask is important. Make sure you ask decision makers, not just your best buddies.

Interviewing Phase

- Are you trying to close an offer too soon?
- Are you still being seen as an outsider which means you are being perceived as having too little inside knowledge about the company or industry you are targeting?

Follow-up phase

- Have you written a follow-up (influencing letter or email) *to everyone* you have talked to? This is one of the most critical things you need to do as it will distinguish you from your competition.

- Are you still nurturing your Stage-1 contacts? This means staying in touch every four weeks.

Dealing With the Lows

Again, we all have our down days but there are some techniques that have withstood the test of time. We suggest you try them. Most would be part of our everyday lives in a perfect world. Somehow the day-to-day stuff of life seems to get in the way but during a serious job search we all need to redouble our efforts to get some of these back into our routines. Many of these are geared to helping you create a positive mental attitude even if just for a few minutes.

- Keep learning. The mind atrophies at an astonishingly fast rate. Learning can be in your professional field, your hobby, something new or a combination.
- Keep in good physical condition. Being in shape is a highly effective stress fighter and the good news is you don't have to become a jock. Remember, the famous cardio specialist, Dr. Cooper found that just 20 minutes of exercise, at your targeted heart rate, three times a week, is all you need for good cardio-vascular health.
- Relaxation. Treat your self every day to some relaxation time. One of the easiest things to do is get up out of your chair for just 5 minutes every hour and take a short walk.
- Program in some fun. Start with your own idea of fun. How do you typically relax? Some clients go back to the Seven Stories Exercise. We even have a few clients who rewrote their Seven Stories but only focused on all the events in their life that were fun. It became the Seven FUN Stories Exercise!

Whether we are talking about golf, ice hockey, wine tasting or a book club . . . you need to keep active at what you enjoy doing.

- Consulting work. It keeps the brain cells active, puts a little bread on the table and creates new contacts but **most important** could lead to a real job.
- Support structure. Family, friends, and networking groups are critical in this process. The key secret here is to communicate how you are doing and where you need help.
- Read motivational literature or listen to motivational tapes or discs. There

are thousands of things available on the web but a good place to start is the Nightingale site: http://www.nightingale.com/

- Tell yourself, *every day*, how truly capable you are and one of the best ways to do this is to write down your business and personal strengths then several things you are thankful for. This sounds hokey but it works.
- Listen to your favorite song or hymn.
- Listen to your favorite school song. Two classics are Michigan and Notre Dame.
- Listen to Ray Charles sing *America the Beautiful*.
- Hug your loved ones, **every day** . . . including the dog and cat!
- Laugh. Laughter and humor are two of the most powerful tools for helping us cope. Fortunately, with the web, there are unlimited sources of humor.

Two of my favorite quotes in this vein are:

Life is too important to be taken seriously. Oscar Wilde

If you can't laugh at yourself . . . well . . . maybe you just aren't funny. Anon.

- Staying active with your volunteering. Not only will it be personally rewarding but it could lead to a job and it will definitely lead to more contacts.

Here is a story about one of our clients who could not stay active in a charity where he was chairman because of the charities' Charter. The Charter stated the chairman had to be employed. However he turned this negative quickly into a positive.

At first he wanted to immediately resign after he lost his job but we urged him to consider another strategy. Why not go to the next board meeting, announce your situation, your intention to step down and offer to help select your successor.

John did just that, and guess what? They really liked his approach. In fact, every executive on the board opened their calendars to set up a meeting with him to discuss his search and to share their networks. He almost fell out of his chair. He ended up with six new Stage-1 contacts and three Stage-2 contacts, all at very senior levels.

A Quick Health, Fitness and Spiritual Audit

Just in case you need a friendly reminder, here are a few questions to ask yourself?

Health

- Are you due for a physical with your primary care physician? Good time to schedule it is **before the new job starts**.

- Do you need to catch up on any medical screening appointments? We find many of our clients put these off when employed.
- Do you sleep enough? Why not? You no longer have to get up at 5AM!
- Are you eating healthy? Snacking healthy?

Fitness

- Are you getting enough exercise? Remember 20 minutes, just three times a week is all you need.
- Can you combine your exercise with fun? A good walk in the park or woods, with your dog, would be a great example.
- Can you combine exercise and volunteering? Teach an exercise class at a senior center.
- Do you need to pay attention to your weight? The majority of companies like to see their executives fit.
- Do you need to hire a fitness trainer? What a great way to break up the day. Have a trainer come to the house for just 30 minutes.

Spiritual

- Are you taking time to fulfill your spiritual needs?
- Think about reconnecting with your Rabbi, Priest or Minister.
- Can you combine spirituality and volunteering? Religious organizations can always use extra hands and minds.
- Can you combine spirituality and relaxation? Meditation is one way.

Chapter Summary

Re-read the above . . . frequently!

12

Mission Accomplished!
Preparing To On-Board

Chapter Overview ....

- Your must do's before your first day on the job
- Your must do's for your first three months

....

"You don't get a job because of what you know. It's about how fast you learn and how much you can adapt" —Jeff Immelt

Congratulations!

You have accepted the right job, at the right company, with the right team.

With the average executive tenure being less than 4 years and dropping the chances are most of you have already undergone a few more job transitions than you would have liked and are quite savvy about how to manage your on-boarding. However it never hurts to double check the basics.

How much time do you have to prepare before your first day on the new job?

When we asked our clients, the responses varied widely. For some it was only one day and for others it was up to four months. The majority fortunately start in two to four weeks but when you factor in a much needed vacation or catching up at home it will not be a lot of time.

So What Are The "Must Do's" or "Must Think About's" Before You Start?

What we are about to share with you is very fundamental but we want to cover it because we have had too many clients tell us after just a few weeks, "I wish I had taken your advice about pulling all my thoughts together before I started. Now I am scrambling to read my interview notes and comments."

First summarize what you know already. In fact, we suggest you do this as soon as you know you are a finalist.

Whether your new company is a start-up, a mature business or a turnaround, the chances are you already have shared many of your preliminary strategic thoughts and vision with your boss and your bosses' boss during the interview process. Has your thought process changed any from those early discussions? If yes, have you written it down? And do you have a plan to communicate it at the appropriate time?

Have you pulled together all your notes so you have them in one document especially the notes on expectations from your boss, and your boss's boss?

If you are moving to a new culture, new country, new function, new industry, or simply a new organization, what norms and values are different from yours and what do you need to do to stay sensitive to those differences?

Having done your due diligence you should have a good feel about the organization and systems in your new company. Will this facilitate or complicate your on-boarding plan?

Are there any gray areas you need to further check out? If yes, do this early.

Hopefully, you have met all of the people on your team but if not that should be a top priority. One of the first things you have to assess quickly, as you well know, is: Can the current team meet the challenges ahead?"

Final TIPS:

1. Create a draft but detailed 30-, 60-, 90-day plan.
2. Sit down with your boss, day one, and review your notes and get buy-in on your preliminary action plans and clarity on your two or three most important deliverables.
3. Try and have a similar meeting with the boss's boss, providing your boss is comfortable with it.

Now That You are On-Board.

According the Center of Creative Leadership, forty percent of senior executive hired from the outside fail within the first 18 months and not because they weren't meeting the numbers. The major cause of failure was they had not cemented the critical personal relationships required to get things done.

There are a number of good books written about on-boarding but we particularly like these: *The New Leader's 100-Day Action Plan* by George Bradt, Jayme A. Check and Jorge Pedraza. *The First Ninety Days* by Michael Watkins and *You're in Charge . . . Now What* by Thomas Neff and James Citrin.

Again, we know you have done this successfully before but we thought a quick refresher wouldn't hurt.

"I'm a little concerned, Randolph. Six of our top competitors have written to thank us for hiring you."

- Be ready for anything. Even if you have done the most thorough due diligence, there will still be surprises. There is no way you will have been able to cover everything. Be ready to completely revisit your hypotheses. Reorganizations and important decisions for your team may have happened between the time you signed your contract and your first day.

- Don't by-pass your introductory meetings and never stop communicating. Find creative ways to organize powerful meetings with your direct reports, peers, other company insiders and even people from the outside (clients, suppliers, etc.). Use your introduction as a way to get their perspectives and give them a flavor of your leadership and communication style.
- **The biggest single trap** is getting into the "do mode" before you have met all the folks who really do the work especially your direct reports. The reason many of us get into the "do mode" is we want to impress the boss and reinforce, "they made the right decision!" It is very normal behavior but unfortunately it has proven fatal to many.
- Your first priority is to immediately begin to build bridges with everyone who can impact your team's success. The good news is, we all start in a honeymoon period so as long as you manage upward well, this step can be accomplished in just a couple of weeks.
- Improve the efficiency of your learning. One of the quickest ways to do this is to know your learning style. Are you a visual learner or auditory? Then let your team and others know it too. This will save you a lot of time because if you are a visual learner and all the reviews are verbal you are going to be frustrated and chances are that frustration will show. Be sure to ask about who the best sources of company information are then talk to them all. They will be flattered and you will be building great bridges!
- Go for the low hanging fruit so you have some early wins. Is there a current situation where you can immediately prove your value (without grandstanding)? Are there areas where you can achieve rapid improvement without a major time or dollar investment? Choose the low hanging fruit based upon the impact on the customers, either internal or external.
- Continually assess your team. Ideally you want a team that complements your skills, and that aligns with your strategy. Become their coach. Hire the competencies that are missing. Don't make decisions too quickly but if you need to make changes, don't be shy.
- Develop a strong working relationship with your boss. How can you best complement each other? How can you best communicate issues, status and successes? How can you best support him or her? Can you shore up their weakness or blind side? Share your preliminary assessment of your team with him and get his feedback.

- Create a strong internal network. Whose support do you need? Who are important and influential people in the organization? Remember the influential are not defined by rank, they are defined by their credibility with the decision makers.
- Work extra hard to build relationships with those who don't support you. This may sound counterintuitive but when you have a healthy relationship with people who oppose your ideas and vise versa, it is much easier to "agree to disagree with respect."
- Don't get stuck on your preliminary strategic agenda. You will usually have several months to craft and finalize it. What is important is that you spend the on-boarding time finding out if you agree with the company's current strategy.
- Learn the thought process behind the current metrics. Are they really what drives the business? Suggest new metrics as appropriate.
- Be very . . . very . . . very cautious if you want to transform the culture. Think about the cultural boundaries of your new organization. Do not try to step out of them too soon. You don't want to become "the rejected organ." At the same time, you can implement small but impactful changes during the first three months, when people in your organization most expect changes to happen.
- Resist becoming a total 24/7 creature. Keep your balance. Keep your personal discipline and healthy lifestyle. Get some help to organize your environment: set up your office, your file management system, and be sure to clarify expectations with your staff.

Final TIPS:

- Communicate with everyone in your network about your new job! Your advisory board should be the first to know, and they will be eager to help you during the transition process.
- Send thank-you notes to those who have helped you during your job search and offer to help them in any way you can.
- If the first three months are going to be like boot-camp let people know. You may have to back off some charity and community commitments. But also communicate it will only be for a few months otherwise you will trap yourself in 24/7 land.

- If you are facing a relocation, decide if your family is going to join you right away. Changing jobs is one of the major life stressors and so is relocation. More and more executives wait for at least 3 months and more often 6 months to see if it makes sense to move.

TIP: Don't let the "school year myth" force a bad decision. The school year myth is, "we have to move before school starts." We all know having our children settled in comfortably is incredibly important. However it's worse to have a double move because the job didn't work out.

Chapter Summary

- Pull together all your notes from the interviews and summarize them into one document as soon as you know you are a finalist.
- In the two to three weeks you have before you start, craft your 90-day plan and go hunting for any information that you might still be missing. This means calling people at the new company. We have found this absolutely impresses the boss. However if it's not well modulated, it will scare the heck out of your subordinates.
- Once on board:
  + Forget anything that you have done so far! Just kidding . . . but be prepared for surprises.
  + Get into the watch and learn mode rather than the do-mode.
  + Go for the low-hanging fruit.
  + Work on your relationships with your boss, direct reports, internal network . . . and especially those who don't support you.
  + When it comes to culture . . . walk on eggs.
  + If relocating, think "three times" before moving your family too quickly.

Hélène and Bill wish you much success!

Appendixes

Exercises to Analyze Your Past and Present: *The Seven Stories Exercise*

The direction of change to seek is not in our four dimensions: it is getting deeper into what you are, where you are, like turning up the volume on the amplifier.
—Thaddeus Golas, *Lazy Man's Guide to Enlightenment*

In this exercise, you will examine your accomplishments, looking at your strongest and most enjoyable skills. The core of most coaching exercises is some version of the Seven Stories Exercise. A coach may give you lots of tests and exercises, but this one requires *work* on your part and will yield the most important results. An interest or personality test is not enough.

Do not skip the Seven Stories Exercise. It will provide you with information for your career direction, your résumé, and your interviews. After you do the exercise, brainstorm about a number of possible job targets. Then research each target to find out what the job possibilities are for someone like you.

If you're like most people, you have never taken the time to sort out the things you're good at and also are motivated to accomplish. As a result, you probably don't use these talents as completely or as effectively as you could. Too often, we do things to please someone else or to survive in a job. Then we get stuck in a rut—that is, we're *always* trying to please someone else or *always* trying to survive in a job. We lose sight of what could satisfy us, and work be-comes drudgery rather than fun. When we become so enmeshed in survival or in trying to please others, it may be difficult to figure out what we would rather be doing.

When you uncover your enjoyable skills, you'll be better able to identify jobs that allow you to use them, and recognize other jobs that don't quite fit the bill. *Enjoyable skills* are patterns that run through our lives. Since they are skills from which we get satisfaction, we'll find ways to do them even if we don't get to do them at work. We still might not know what these skills are—for us, they're just something we do, and we take them for granted. That's why you should ask other people—your parents and friends—what they see as your enjoyable skills.

Tracking down these patterns takes some thought. The payoff is that our enjoyable skills do not change. They run throughout our lives and indicate what will keep us motivated for the rest of our lives.

Look at Donald Trump. He knows that he enjoys—and is good at—real estate and self-promotion, and that's what he concentrates on. Now remember that you may have 3 to 5 different careers throughout your life—not 3 to 5 jobs, but 3 to 5 *careers*. Still, you can identify commonalities in those careers—aspects that you must have that will make you happier and more successful. In my case, for example, whether I was a computer programmer, a chief financial officer or a career coach, I've always found a way to teach others and often ran small groups—even in my childhood!

You too will find commonalities in your accomplishments, and these may be indicators of the elements you need in a job to be happier and more successful. Let's take one more example. An accountant whose enjoyable accomplishments involve helping the business head and giving advice would probably not be happy sitting in a corner crunching numbers and getting the numbers to balance. If what motivates him is the helping part, then he must be in a job where he is helping—perhaps giving advice to clients. Chances are, this person enjoyed helping people even when he was very young and this is a pattern that runs through many of his accomplishments.

One's prime is elusive. . . . You must be on the alert to recognize your prime at whatever time of life it may occur. —Muriel Spark, *The Prime of Miss Jean Brodie*

The Seven Stories Approach: Background

This technique for identifying what people do well and enjoy doing has its roots in the work of Bernard Haldane, Ph.D, who in the 1940s, helped military personnel transition their skills to civilian life. Its overwhelming success in this area won the attention of Harvard Business School where it went on to become a significant part of its *Manual for Alumni Placement*. Haldane's work is being carried on today by practitioners of the Dependable Strengths Articulation Process (DSAP) all over the world through the Center for Dependable Strengths in Seattle, WA. The volunteers of this non-profit public charity have brought Haldane's methods to places as diverse as South Africa and China, to colleges and universities, public education, churches, social service agencies and in their work with people of all ages.

The exercise is this: Make a list of all the enjoyable accomplishments of your life, those things you enjoyed doing *and also* did well. List at least 25 enjoyable accomplishments from all parts of your life: work, from your youth, your school years, your early career up to the present. Don't forget volunteer work, your hobbies and your personal life. Other people may have gotten credit or under-appreciated what you did. Or the result may not have been a roaring success. For example, perhaps you were assigned to develop a new product and take it to market. Let's say you worked on this project for two years, loved every minute of it, but it failed in the market. It doesn't matter. What matters is that you enjoyed doing it and did it well.

Examine those episodes that gave you a sense of accomplishment. You are asked to name 25 accomplishments so you will not be too judgmental—just list anything that occurs to you. Don't expect to sit down and think of everything. Expect to think of enjoyable accomplishments over the course of four or five days. Be sure to ask others to help you think of your accomplishments. Most people carry around a piece of paper so they can jot ideas down as they occur to them. When you have 25, select the seven that are most important to you by however you define important. Then rank them: List the most important first, and so on.

Starting with your first story, write a paragraph about each accomplishment. Then find out what your accomplishments have in common. If you are having trouble doing the exercises, ask a friend to help you talk them through. Friends tend to be more objective and will probably point out strengths you never realized.

You will probably be surprised. For example, you may be especially good interacting with people, but it's something you've always done and therefore take for granted. This may be a pattern that runs through your life and may be one of your enjoyable skills. It *may* be that you'll be unhappy in a job that doesn't allow you to deal with people.

When I did the Seven Stories Exercise, one of the first stories I listed was from when I was 10 years old, when I wrote a play to be put on by the kids in the neighborhood. I rehearsed everyone, sold tickets to the adults for two cents apiece, and served cookies and milk with the proceeds. You might say that my direction as a *general manager*—running the whole show, thinking things up, getting everybody working together—was set in the fourth grade. I saw these traits over and over again in each of my stories.

After I saw those patterns running through my life, it became easy for me to see what elements a job must have to satisfy me. When I interview for a job, I can find out in short order whether it addresses my enjoyable skills. If it doesn't, I won't be as happy as I could be, even though I *may decide to take the job as an interim step toward a long-term goal.* The fact is, people won't do as well *in the long run* in jobs that don't satisfy their enjoyable skills.

Sometimes I don't pay attention to my own enjoyable skills, and I wind up doing things I regret. For example, in high school I scored the highest in the state in math. I was as surprised as everyone else, but I felt I finally had some direction in my life. I felt I had to use it to do some-thing constructive. When I went to college, I majored in math. I almost flunked because I was bored with it. The fact is that I didn't *enjoy* math, I was simply good at it.

There are lots of things we're good at, but they may not be the same things we really enjoy. The trick is to find those things we are good at, enjoy doing, and feel a sense of accomplishment from doing.

To sum up: Discovering your enjoyable skills is the first step in career planning. I was a general manager when I was 10, but I didn't realize it. I'm a general manager now, and I love it. In between, I've done some things that have helped me toward my long-range goals, and other things that have not helped at all.

It is important to realize that the Seven Stories Exercise will *not* tell you exactly which job you should have, but the *elements* to look for in a job that you will find satisfying. You'll have a range of jobs to consider, and you'll know the elements the jobs must have to keep you happy. Once you've selected a few job categories that might satisfy you, talk to people in those fields to find out if a particular job is really what you want, and the job possibilities for someone with your experience. That's one way to test if your aspirations are realistic.

After you have narrowed your choices down to a few fields with some job possibilities that will satisfy your enjoyable skills, the next step is to figure out how to get there. That topic will be covered in our book *Shortcut Your Job Search*.

> . . . *be patient toward all that is unsolved in your heart and try to love the questions themselves like locked rooms and like books that are written in a foreign tongue.*
> —Rainer Maria Rilke, *Letters to a Young Poet*

A Demonstration of the Seven Stories Exercise

To get clients started, I sometimes walk them through two or three of their enjoyable accomplishments, and tell them the patterns I see. They can then go off and think of the seven or eight accomplishments they enjoyed the most and also performed well. This final list is ranked and analyzed in depth to get a more accurate picture of the person's enjoyable skills. I spend the most time analyzing those accomplishments a client sees as most important. Some accomplishments are more obvious than others. But all stories can be analyzed.

Here is Suzanne, as an example: "When I was nine years old, I was living with my three sisters. There was a fire in our house and our cat had hidden under the bed. We were all outside, but I decided to run back in and save the cat. And I did it."

No matter what the story is, I probe a little by asking questions: What was the accomplishment for you? and What about that made you proud? These questions give me a quick fix on the person.

The full exercise is a little more involved than this. Suzanne said at first: "I was proud because I did what I thought was right." I probed a little, and she added: "The accomplishment was that I was able to make an instant decision under pressure. I was proud because I overcame my fear."

I asked Suzanne for a second story; I wanted to see what patterns might emerge when we put the two together: "Ten years ago, I was laid off from a large company where I had worked for nine years.

I soon got a job as a secretary in a Wall Street company. I loved the excitement and loved that job. Six weeks later, a position opened up on the trading floor, but I didn't get it at first. I eventually was one of three finalists, and they tried to discourage me from taking the job. I wanted to be given a chance. So I sold myself because I was determined to get that job. I went back for three interviews, said all the right things, and eventually got it."

- "I fought to win."
- "I was able to sell myself. I was able to overcome their objections."
- "I was interviewed by three people at once. I amazed myself by saying, 'I know I can do this job.'"
- "I determined who the real decision maker was, and said things that would make him want to hire me."
- "I loved that job—loved the energy, the upness, the fun."

Here it was, 10 years later, and that job still stood out as a highlight in her life. Since then she'd been miserable and bored, and that's why she came to me.

Normally after a client tells two stories, we can quickly name the patterns we see in both stories. What were Suzanne's patterns?

Suzanne showed that she was good at making decisions in tense situations—both when saving the cat and when interviewing for that job. She showed a good intuitive sense (such as when she determined who the decision maker was and how to win him over). She's decisive and likes fast-paced, energetic situations. She likes it when she overcomes her own fears as well as the objections of others.

What was the accomplishment?

What made her proud?

We needed more than two stories to see if these patterns ran throughout Suzanne's life and to see what other patterns might emerge. After the full exercise, Suzanne felt for sure that she wanted excitement in her jobs, a sense of urgency—that she wanted to be in a position where she had a chance to be decisive and operate intuitively. Those are the conditions she enjoys and under which she operates the best.

Armed with this information, Suzanne can confidently say in an interview that she thrives on excitement, high pressure, and quick decision-making. And, she'll probably make more money than she would in *safe* jobs. She can move her life in a different direction—whenever she is ready.

Pay attention to those stories that were most important to you. The elements in these stories may be worth repeating. If none of your enjoyable accomplishments were work related, it may take great courage to eventually move into a field where you will be happier. Or you may decide to continue to have your enjoyment outside of work.

People have to be ready to change. Fifteen years ago, when I first examined my own enjoyable skills, I saw possibilities I was not ready to handle. Although I suffered from extreme shyness, my stories—especially those that occurred when I was young—gave me hope. As I emerged from my shyness, I was eventually able to act on what my stories said was true about me.

People sometimes take immediate steps after learning what their enjoyable skills are. Or sometimes this new knowledge can work inside them until they are ready to take action—maybe 10 years later. All the while internal changes can be happening, and people can eventually blossom.

If one advances confidently in the direction of his dreams, and endeavors to live the life which he has imagined, he will meet with success unexpected in common hours.
—Henry David Thoreau

Enjoyable Skills—Your Anchor in a Changing World

Your enjoyable skills are your anchor in a world of uncertainty. The world will change, but your enjoyable skills remain constant.

Write them down. Save the list. Over the years, refer to them to make sure you are still on target—doing things that you do well and are motivated to do. As you refer to them, they will influence your life. Five years from now, an opportunity may present itself. In reviewing your list, you will have every confidence that this opportunity is right for you. After all, you have been doing these things since you were a child, you know that you enjoy them, and you do them well!

Knowing our patterns gives us a sense of stability and helps us understand what we have done so far. It also gives us the freedom to try new things regard-less of risk or of what others may say, because we can be absolutely sure that this is the way we are. Knowing your patterns gives you both security and flexibility—and you need both to cope in this changing world. Now think about your own stories. Write down everything that occurs to you.

The Ugly Duckling was so happy and in some way he was glad that he had experienced so much hardship and misery; for now he could fully appreciate his tremendous luck and the great beauty that greeted him. . . . And he rustled his feathers, held his long neck high, and with deep emotion he said: "I never dreamt of so much happiness, when I was the Ugly Duckling!" —Hans Christian Anderson, *The Ugly Duckling*

The Seven Stories Exercise™ Worksheet

This exercise is an opportunity to examine the most satisfying experiences of your life and to discover those skills you will want to use as you go forward. You will be looking at the times when you feel you did something particularly well that you also enjoyed doing. Complete this sentence: "There was a time when I . . ." List enjoyable accomplishments from all parts of your life: from your youth, your school years, your early career up to the present. Don't forget volunteer work, your hobbies and your personal life. Other people may have gotten credit or under-appreciated what you did. Or the result may not have been a roaring success. None of that matters. What matters is that you enjoyed doing it and did it well.

List anything that occurs to you, however insignificant. When I did my own Seven Stories Exercise, I remembered the time when I was 10 years old and led a group of kids in the neighborhood, enjoyed it, and did it well.

When you have 25, select the seven that are most important to you by however you define important. Then rank them: List the most important first, and so on. Starting with your first story, write a paragraph about each accomplishment. Then find out what your accomplishments have in common. If you are having trouble doing the exercises, ask a friend to help you talk them through. Friends tend to be more objective and will probably point out strengths you never realized.

Section I

Briefly outline below *all* the work/personal/life experiences that meet the above definition. Come up with at least 20. We ask for 20 stories so you won't be too selective. Just write down anything that occurs to you, no matter how insignificant it may seem. Complete this sentence, "There was a time when I . . ." You may start with, for example, "Threw a fiftieth birthday party for my father," "Wrote a press release that resulted in extensive media coverage," and "Came in third in the Nassau bike race."

Don't just write that you enjoy "cooking." That's an *activity,* not an accomplishment. An accomplishment occurs at a specific time. You may wind up with *many* cooking accomplishments, for example. But if you simply write "cooking," "writing" or "managing," you will have a hard time thinking of 20 enjoyable accomplishments.

1. _____
2. _____
3. _____
4. _____
5. _____
6. _____
7. _____
8. _____
9. _____
10. _____
11. _____
12. _____
13. _____
14. _____
15. _____
16. _____
17. _____
18. _____
19. _____
20. _____

21. _____
22. _____
23. _____
24. _____
25. _____

Section II

Choose the seven experiences from the above that you enjoyed the most and felt the most sense of accomplishment about. (Be sure to include non-job-related experiences also.) Then **rank them.** Then, for each accomplishment, describe what *you* did. Be specific, listing each step in detail. Use a separate sheet of paper for each.

If your highest-ranking accomplishments also happen to be work related, you may want them to appear prominently on your résumé. After all, those were things that you enjoyed and did well. And those are probably experiences you will want to repeat again in your new job.

Here's how you might begin:

Experience #1: Planned product launch that resulted in 450 letters of intent from 1,500 participants.

   a. Worked with president and product managers to discuss product potential and details.

   b. Developed promotional plan.

   c. Conducted five-week direct-mail campaign prior to conference to create aura of excitement about product.

   d. Trained all product demonstrators to make sure they each presented product in same way.

   e. Had great product booth built; rented best suite to entertain prospects; conducted campaign at conference by having teasers put under everyone's door every day of conference. Most people wanted to come to our booth.

—and so on—

Analyzing Your Seven Stories

Now it is time to analyze your stories. You are trying to look for the patterns that run through them so that you will know the things you do well that also give you satisfaction. Some of the questions below sound similar. That's okay. They are a catalyst to make you think more deeply about the experience. The questions don't have any hidden psychological significance.

If your accomplishments happen to be mostly work related, this exercise will form the basis for your *positioning* or summary statement in your résumé, and also for your Two-Minute Pitch. If these accomplishments are mostly not work related, they will still give you some idea of how you may want to slant your résumé, and they may give you an idea of how you will want your career to go in the long run.

For now, simply go through each story without trying to force it to come out any particular way. Just think hard about yourself. And be as honest as you can. When you have completed this analysis, the words in the next exercise may help you think of additional things. **Do this page first.**

Story #1. _____

What was the *accomplishment?*_____

_____

What about it did you *enjoy most?* _____

_____

What did you *do best?* _____

_____

What *motivated you to do this?* _____

_____

What about it *made you proud?* _____

_____

What *prompted you to do this?* _____

_____

What *enjoyable skills did you demonstrate?* _____

_____

Story #2._____

The accomplishment? _____

Enjoyed most? _____

Did best?_____

A motivator? _____

Made you proud? _____

Prompted you to do this? _____

Enjoyable skills demonstrated?_____

Story #3._____

The accomplishment? _____

Enjoyed most? _____

Did best?_____

A motivator? _____

Made you proud? _____

Prompted you to do this? _____

Enjoyable skills demonstrated?_____

Story #4._____

The accomplishment? _____

Enjoyed most? _____

Did best?_____

A motivator? _____

Made you proud? _____

Prompted you to do this? _____

Enjoyable skills demonstrated?_____

Story #5._____

The accomplishment? _____

Enjoyed most? _____

Did best?_____

A motivator? _____

Made you proud? _____

Prompted you to do this? _____

Enjoyable skills demonstrated?_____

Story #6._____

The accomplishment? _____

Enjoyed most? _____

Did best?_____

A motivator? _____

Made you proud? _____

Prompted you to do this? _____

Enjoyable skills demonstrated?_____

Story #7. _____

The accomplishment? _____

Enjoyed most? _____

Did best?_____

A motivator? _____

Made you proud? _____

Prompted you to do this? _____

Enjoyable skills demonstrated?_____

We are here to be excited from youth to old age, to have an insatiable curiosity about the world. . . We are also here to help others by practicing a friendly attitude. And every person is born for a purpose. Everyone has a God-given potential, in essence, built into them. And if we are to live life to its fullest, we must realize that potential. —Norman Vincent Peale

How To Decide
What You Want

What seems different in yourself; that's the rare thing you possess. The one thing that gives each of us his worth, and that's just what we try to suppress. And we claim to love life. —André Gide

Looking Ahead—A Career Instead of a Job

If you don't decide where you want to go, you may wind up drifting from one organization to another whenever you're dissatisfied, with pretty much the same job each time. Even if you decide that you want to continue doing what you're doing right now, that's a goal in itself and may be difficult to achieve.

The first step in career management is goal setting. There are a lot of processes involved in the goal-setting area. But the one considered most cen-tral is that by which a person examines his or her past accomplishments, look-ing at the strongest and most enjoyable skills.

This process is not only the one favored by coaches, it is also the one most often used by successful people. In reading the biographies of such people, I see again and again how they established their goals by identifying those things they enjoy doing and also do well. This process of identifying your *enjoy-able accomplishments* is the most important one you can go through.

What Successful People Do

When Steven Jobs, the founder of Apple Computers, was fired by John Sculley, the man he had brought in to run the company, he felt as though he had lost everything. Apple had been his life. Now he had lost not only his job, but his company. People no longer felt the need to return his phone calls. He did what a lot of us would do. He got depressed. But then:

> *Confused about what to do next . . . he [Jobs] put himself through an exercise that management psychologists employ with clients unsure about their life goals. It was a little thing, really. It was just a list. A list of all the things that mattered most to Jobs during his ten years at Apple. "Three things jumped off that piece of paper, three things that were really important to me," says Jobs.* —Michael Meyer, *The Alexander Complex*

> *Let me listen to me and not to them.* —Gertrude Stein

The exercise Steven Jobs went through is essentially what you will do in the Seven Stories Exercise. The patterns that ran through his stories formed the impetus for his next great drive: the formation of NeXT computers. If the Seven Stories Exercise is good enough for Steven Jobs, maybe it's good enough for you.

"Successful managers," says Charles Garfield, head of Performance Services,

Inc., in Berkeley, California, "go with their preferences." They search for work that is important to them, and when they find it they pursue it with a passion.

Lester Korn, chairman of Korn, Ferry, notes in his book *The Success Profile:* "Few executives know, or can know, exactly what they aspire to until they have been in the work force for a couple of years. It takes that long to learn enough about yourself to know what you can do well and what will make you happy. The trick is to merge the two into a goal, then set off in pursuit of it."

Our book, Targeting a Great Career," will help you decide what you want to do in your next job as well as in the long run. You will become more clear about the experiences you have enjoyed most and may like to repeat. You will also ex-amine your interests and values, and look at past positions to analyze what satisfied you and what did not. In addition, you will look farther ahead (through your Forty-Year Vision) to see if some driving dream may influence what you will want to do in the short term. I did my Forty-Year Vision many years ago, and the vision I had of my future still drives me today.

Knowing where you would like to wind up broadens the kinds of jobs you would be interested in today.

Look at it this way:

The line represents your life. Right now, you are at A. Your next job is B. If you look only at your past to decide what to do next, your next job is limited by what you have already done. For example, if you have been in finance and accounting for the past 15 years, and you base your next move on your past, your next job is likely to be in finance or accounting.

If you know that at C you would like to wind up as vice president of finance and administration, new possibilities open up. Think of all the areas you would manage:

- Finance
- Administration
- Accounting
- Operations
- Human Resources
- IT

Experience in any one of these would advance your career in the right direction. For example, you may decide to get some computer experience.

Without the benefit of a Forty-Year Vision, a move to computers might look like the start of a career in computers, but *you* know it's just one more assignment that leads to your long-term goal. You'll keep your vision in mind and take jobs and assignments that will continually position you for the long run. For example, in the computer area, you may focus on personnel or administrative systems, two areas that fit your goal. Then your computer job will be more than a job. You will work hard for your employer, but you will also know why you are there—you are using your job as a stepping-stone to something bigger and better.

Make no little plans; they have no magic to stir men's blood and probably themselves will not be realized. Make big plans; aim high in hope and work. —Daniel Burnham

Happy in Your Work

People are happy when they are working toward their goals. When they get diverted—or don't know what their goals are—they are unhappy. Many people are unhappy in their jobs because they don't know where they are going. People without goals are more irked by petty daily problems than are those with goals.

To control your life, know where you are going, and be ready for your next move—in case the ax falls on you. When you take that next job, continue to manage your career. Companies rarely build career paths for their employees any more. Make your own way. There are plenty of jobs for those who are willing to learn and to change with the times.

Your Fifteen-Year Vision® and Your Forty-Year Vision®

In my practice as a psychiatrist, I have found that helping people to develop personal gains has proved to be the most effective way to help them cope with problems. —Ari Kiev, M.D., A Strategy for Daily Living

If you could imagine your ideal life five years from now, what would it be like? How would it be different from the way it is now? If you made new friends during the next five years, what would they be like? Where would you be living? What would your hobbies and interests be? How about 10 years from now? Twenty? Thirty? Forty? Think about it!

Some people feel locked in by their present circumstances. Many say it is too late for them. But a lot can happen in 5, 10, 20, 30, or 40 years. Reverend King had a dream. His dream helped all of us, but his dream helped him too. He was living according to a vision (which he thought was God's plan for him). *It gave him a purpose in life.* Most successful people have a vision.

A lot can happen to you over the next few decades—and most of what happens is up to you. If you see the rest of your life as boring, I'm sure you will be right. Some people pick the "sensible" route or the one that fits in with how others see them, rather than the one that is best for them.

On the other hand, you can come up with a few scenarios of how your life could unfold. In that case, you will have to do a lot of thinking and a lot of research to figure out which path makes most sense for you and will make you happiest.

When a person finds a vision that is right, the most common reaction is fear. It is often safer to *wish* a better life than to actually go after it.

I know what that's like. It took me two years of thinking and research to figure out the right path for myself—one that included my motivated abilities (Seven Stories Exercise) as well as the sketchy vision I had for myself. Then it took *10 more years* to finally take the plunge and commit to that path—running The Five O'Clock Club. I was 40 years old when I finally took a baby step in the right direction, and I was terrified.

You may be lucky and find it easy to write out your vision of your future.

Or you may be more like me: It may take a while and a lot of hard work. You can speed up the process by reviewing your assessment results with a Five O'Clock Club career counselor. He or she will guide you along. Remember, when I was struggling, the country didn't *have* Five O'Clock Club counselors or even these exercises to guide us.

Test your vision and see if that path seems right for you. Plunge in by researching it and meeting with people in the field. If it is what you want, chances are you will find some way to make it happen. If it is not exactly right, you can modify it later—after you have gathered more information and perhaps gotten more experience.

Start with the Present

Write down, in the present tense, the way your life is right now, and the way you see yourself at each of the time frames listed. **This exercise should take no more than one hour.** Allow your unconscious to tell you what you will be doing in the future. Just quickly comment on each of the questions listed on the following page, and then move on to the next. If you kill yourself off too early (say, at age 60), push it 10 more years to see what would have happened if you had lived. Then push it another 10, just for fun.

When you have finished the exercise, ask yourself how you feel about your entire life as you laid it out in your vision. Some people feel depressed when they see on paper how their lives are going, and they cannot think of a way out. But they feel better when a good friend or a Five O'Clock Club counselor helps them think of a better future to work toward. If you don't like your vision, you are allowed to change it—it's your life. Do what you want with it. Pick the kind of life you want.

Start the exercise with the way things are now so you will be realistic about your future. Now, relax and have a good time going through the years. Don't think too hard. Let's see where you wind up. You have plenty of time to get things done.

The 15-year mark proves to be the most important for most people. It's far enough away from the present to allow you to dream.

There are more things in heaven and earth, Horatio, then are dreamt of in your philosophy. —William Shakespeare, *Hamlet*

Your Fifteen- and Forty-Year-Vision Worksheet

1. The year is_____ (*current year*).
   You are _____ years old right now.

• Tell me what your life is like right now. (*Say anything you want about your life as it is now.*)

   _____
   _____
   _____

• Who are your friends? What do they do for a living?

   _____
   _____

• What is your relationship with your family, however you define "family"?

   _____

• Are you married? Single? Children? (*list ages*)

   _____
   _____

• Where are you living? What does it look like?

   _____
   _____

• What are your hobbies and interests?

   _____
   _____

• What do you do for exercise?

   _____

• How is your health?

   _____

• How do you take care of your spiritual needs?

   _____

• What kind of work are you doing?

   _____

• What else would you like to note about your life right now?

   _____

Don't worry if you don't like everything about your life right now. Most people do this exercise because they want to improve themselves. They want to change something? What do you want to change?

Five Years

2. The year is _____ (*current year 5*).
You are _____ years old. (*Add 5 to present age.*)

Things are going well for you.

* What is your life like now at this age? (*Say anything you want about your life as it is now.*)

  _____

  _____

* Who are your friends? What do they do for a living?

  _____

  _____

* What is your relationship with your "family"?

  _____

* Married? Single? Children? (*List their ages now.*)

  _____

* Where are you living? What does it look like?

  _____

  _____

* What are your hobbies and interests?

  _____

* What do you do for exercise?

  _____

* How is your health?

  _____

* How do you take care of your spiritual needs?

  _____

* What kind of work are you doing?

  _____

* What else would you like to note about your life right now?

  _____

  _____

Fifteen Year

3. The year is _____ *(current year 15)*.
   You are _____ years old. *(Current age plus 15.)*

- What is your life like now at this age? *(Say anything you want about your life as it is now.)*
  _____
  _____

- Who are your friends? What do they do for a living?
  _____

- What is your relationship with your "family"?
  _____

- Married? Single? Children? *(List their ages now.)*
  _____

- Where are you living? What does it look like?
  _____
  _____

- What are your hobbies and interests?
  _____

- What do you do for exercise?
  _____

- How is your health?
  _____

- How do you take care of your spiritual needs?
  _____

- What kind of work are you doing?
  _____

- What else would you like to note about your life right now?
  _____
  _____
  _____

The 15-year mark is an especially important one. This age is far enough away from the present that people often loosen up a bit. It's so far away that it's not threatening. Imagine your ideal life. What is it like? Why were you put here on this earth? What were you meant to do here? What kind of life were you meant to live? Give it a try and see what you come up with. If you can't think of anything now, try it again in a week or so. On the other hand, if you got to the 15-year mark, why not keep going?

Twenty-fifth Year

4. The year is _____ (*current year 25*).

    You are _____ years old! (*Current age plus 25.*)

Using a blank sheet of paper, aanswer all the questions from previous worksheets for this stage of your life.

5. The year is _____ (*current year 35*).

You are _____ years old! (*Current age plus 35.*)

Using a blank sheet of paper, aanswer all the questions from previous worksheets for this stage of your life.

6. The year is _____ (*current year 45*).

You are _____ years old!

Using a blank sheet of paper, aanswer all the questions from previous worksheets for this stage of your life.

(*Current age plus 45.*)

7. The year is _____ (*current year 55*).

You are _____ years old! (*Current age plus 55.*)

Using a blank sheet of paper, aanswer all the questions from previous worksheets for this stage of your life.

Keep going—don't die until you are past 80!

How do you feel about your life? You are allowed to change the parts you don't like.

You have plenty of time to get done everything you want to do. Imagine wonderful things for yourself. You have plenty of time. Get rid of any "negative programming." For example, if you imagine yourself having poor health because your parents suffered from poor health, see what you can do about that. If you imagine yourself dying early because that runs in your family, see what would have happened had you lived longer. It's your life—your only one. As they say, "This is the real thing. It's not a dress rehearsal."

Case Study:
Howard: Developing A Vision

In the thick of active life, there is more need to stimulate fancy than to control it.
—George Santayana, *The Life of Reason*

Howard attended a Five O'Clock Club group that specializes in helping people who are not yet in professional-level jobs. He had done the Seven Stories and other exercises and had tried to do the Forty-Year Vision. Like most people, he had left out important parts, such as what he could be doing for a living. That's okay. I asked him if he would mind doing it in the small discussion group.

At the time, Howard was 35 years old and worked in a lower-level job in the advertising industry. He wanted to advance in his career by getting another job in advertising. Based on our research into the jobs of the future, which showed that this current industry was a shaky choice, we asked him to postpone selecting an industry while we helped him complete his Forty-Year Vision.

HAPPY: All I can do now is wait for the merchandise manager to die. And suppose I get to be merchandise manager? He's a good friend of mine, and he just built a terrific estate on Long Island. And he lived there about two months and sold it, and now he's building another one. He can't enjoy it once it's finished. And I know that's just what I would do. I don't know what the hell I'm workin' for. —Arthur Miller, Death of a Salesman

Howard was just getting started on his career even though he was 35. You're just getting started too. Regardless of your age, take pen to paper and force yourself to write something. You can always change it later.

Filling in His Forty-Year Vision

Kate: "Howard, you're 35 years old right now. Tell me: Who are your friends and what do they do for a living?"

Howard: "John is a messenger; Keith minds the kids while his wife works; and Greg delivers food."

Kate: "What do you do for a living?"

Howard: "I work in the media department of an advertising agency."

Kate: "Okay. Now, let's go out a few years. You're 40 years old, and you've made a number of new friends in the past five years. Who are these people? What are they doing for a living?"

Howard: "One friend is a medical doctor; another works in finance or for the stock exchange; and a third is in a management position in the advertising industry."

Kate: "That's fine. Now, let's go out further. You're 50 years old, and you have made a lot of new friends. What are they doing for a living?"

Howard: "One is an executive managing 100 to 200 people in a corporation and is very well respected; a second one is in education—he's the principal or the administrator of an experimental high school and gets written up in the newspapers all the time; a third is a vice president in finance or banking."

Kate: "Those are important-sounding friends you have Howard. But who are you and what are you doing that these people are associating with you?"

Howard: "I'm not sure."

Kate: "Well, how much money are you making at age 50 in today's dollars?"

Howard: "I'm making $150,000 a year."

Kate: "I'm impressed. What are you doing to earn that kind of money, Howard? What kind of place are you working in? Remember, you don't *have* to be specific about the industry or field you're in. For example, how do you dress for work?"

Howard: "I wear a suit and tie every day. I have a staff of 60 people working for me: six departments, with 10 people in each department."

Kate: "And what are those people doing all day?"

Howard: "They're doing paperwork, or computer work."

Kate: "That's great, Howard. We now have a pretty good idea of what you'll be doing in the future. We just need to fill in some details." I said to the group: "Perhaps Howard won't be making $150,000, but he'll certainly be making a lot by his own standards. And maybe it won't be 60 people, but it will certainly be a good-sized staff. What Howard is talking about here is a concept. The details may be wrong, but the concept is correct."

If I see what I want real good in my mind, I don't notice any pain in getting it.

George Foreman, former heavyweight boxing champion of the world

Howard: "But I'm not sure if that's what I really want to do."

Kate: "It may not be exactly what you want to do, Howard, but it's in the right direction and contains the elements you really want. What you just said fits in with your Seven Stories exercise (one story was about your work with computers; another was about an administrative accomplishment). Think about it for the next week, but I'll tell you this: You won't decide you want to be a dress designer, like Roxanne here. Nor will you say you want to sell insurance, like Barry. What you will do will be very close to what you just described.

"If you come back next week and say that you've decided to sell ice cream, for example, I'll tell you that you simply became afraid. Fear often keeps people form pursuing their dreams. Over the week, read about the jobs of the future, and let me know the industries you may want to investigate for your future career. It's usually better to pick growth industries rather than declining ones. You stand a better chance of rising with the tide."

The Next Week

When it was Howard's turn in the group the next week, he announced that he had selected health care as the industry he wanted to investigate. That sounded good because it is a growth field and because there will be plenty of need for someone to manage a group of people working on computers.

We brainstormed the areas within health care that Howard could research. He could work in a hospital, an HMO, a health-care association, and so on. He could learn about the field by reading the trade magazines having to do with health care administration, and he could start networking by meeting with someone else in the group who had already worked in a hospital.

Week #3

Howard met with the other person in the group and got a feel for what it was like to work in a hospital. He also got a few names of people he could talk to—people at his level who could give him basic information. He had spent some time in a library reading trade magazines having to do with health-care administration.

Howard needed to do a lot more research before he would be ready to meet with higher-level people—those in a position to hire him.

Week #4

Howard announced to the group that he had done more research, which helped him figure out that he would start in the purchasing area of a hospital, as opposed to the financial area, for example. In previous jobs, he had worked both as a buyer and as a salesman, so he knew both sides of the picture. He would spend some time researching the purchasing aspect of health care. That could be his entry point, and he could make other moves after he got into the field.

A human being certainly would not grow to be seventy or eighty years old if his longevity had no meaning for the species. —C. G. Jung

Week #5

Today Howard is ready to meet with higher-level people in the health-care field. As he networks around, he will learn even more about the field, and select the job and the organization that will position him best for the long run—the situation that fits in best with his Forty-Year Vision.

After Howard gets his next job, he will occasionally come to the group to ask the others to help him think about his career and make moves within the organization. He will be successful in living his vision if he continues to do what needs to be done, never taking his eye off the ball.

If Howard sticks with his vision, he will make good money, and live in the kind of place in which he wants to live. Like many people who develop written plans, Howard has the opportunity to have his dreams come true.

You can either say the universe is totally random and it's just molecules colliding all the time and it's totally chaos and our job is to make sense of that chaos, or you can say sometimes things happen for a reason and your job is to discover the reason. But either way, I do see it meaning an opportunity and that has made all the difference. —Christopher Reeve, former star of *Superman,* in an interview with Barbara Walters. Reeve became a quadriplegic after a horseback-riding accident.

You Can Do It Too

As I mentioned earlier, the group that Howard attended is a special Five O'Clock Club program that works mostly with adults who are not yet in the professional or managerial ranks, and helps them get into professional-track jobs. For example:

Emlyn, a 35-year-old former babysitter, embarked on and completed a program to become a nurse's aide. This is her first step toward becoming an R.N., her ultimate career goal.

Calvin, who suffers form severe rheumatoid arthritis, hadn't worked in 10 years. Within five weeks of starting with us, he got a job as a consumer advocate with a center for the disabled, and has a full caseload. We are continuing to work with him.

These ambitious, hard-working people did it, and so can you. It's not easy, but what else are you doing with your 24 hours a day? The people who did it followed this motto: "Have a dream. Make a plan. Take a step. Keep on climbing."

You can complain that you haven't gotten lucky breaks, but Howard, Emlyn, and Calvin didn't either.

They made their own breaks, attended a branch of The Five O'Clock Club, and kept plugging ahead despite difficulties. If they can do it, you can do it too.

What Is The Five O'Clock Club?

America's Premier
Career-coaching
Network

How To Join The Club

The Five O'Clock Club:
America's Premier Career-Coaching and Outplacement Service

"One organization with a long record of success in helping people find jobs is The Five O'Clock Club." —Fortune

- Job-Search Strategy Groups
- Private Coaching
- Books and Audio CDs
- Membership Information
- When Your Employer Pays

THERE *IS* A FIVE O'CLOCK CLUB NEAR YOU!
For more information on becoming a member, please fill out the Membership Application Form in this book, sign up on the web at: www.fiveoclockclub.com, or call: 1-800-575-3587 (or 212-286-4500 in New York)

The Five O'Clock Club Search Process

The Five O'Clock Club process, as outlined in *The Five O'Clock Club* books, is a targeted, strategic approach to career development and job search. Five O'Clock Club members become proficient at skills that prove invaluable during their *entire working lives*.

Career Management

We train our members to *manage their careers* and always look ahead to their next job search. Research shows that an average worker spends only four years in a job—and will have 12 jobs in as many as 5 career fields—during his or her working life.

Getting Jobs . . . Faster

Five O'Clock Club members find *better jobs, faster.* The average professional, manager, or executive Five O'Clock Club member who regularly attends weekly sessions finds a job by his or her 10th session. Even the discouraged, long-term job searcher can find immediate help.

The keystone to The Five O'Clock Club process is teaching our members an understanding of the entire hiring process. A first interview is primarily a time for exchanging critical information. The real work starts *after* the interview. We teach our members *how to turn job interviews into offers* and to negotiate the best possible employment package.

Setting Targets

The Five O'Clock Club is action oriented. *We'll help you decide what you should do this very next week to move your search along.* By their third session, our members have set definite job targets by industry or company size, position, and geographic area, and are out in the field gathering information and making contacts that will lead to interviews with hiring managers.

Our approach evolves with the changing job market. We're able to synthesize information from hundreds of Five O'Clock Club members and come up with new approaches for our members. For example, we now discuss temporary placement for executives, how to use voice mail and the Internet, and how to network when doors are slamming shut all over town.

The Five O'Clock Club Strategy Program

The Five O'Clock Club meeting is a carefully planned *job-search strategy program.* We provide members with the tools and tricks necessary to get a good job fast—even in a tight market. Networking and emotional support are also included in the meeting. Participate in 10 *consecutive* small-group strategy sessions to enable your group and career coach to get to know you and to develop momentum in your search.

Weekly Presentations via Audio CDs

Prior to each week's teleconference, listen to the assigned audio presentation covering part of The Five O'Clock Club methodology. These are scheduled on a rotating basis so you may join the Club at any time. (In selected cities, presentations are given in person rather than via audio CDs.)

Small-Group Strategy Sessions

During the first few minutes of the teleconference, your small group discusses the topic of the week and hears from people who have landed jobs. Then you have the chance to get feedback and advice on your own search strategy, listen to and learn from others, and build your network. All groups are led by trained career coaches with years of experience. The small group is generally no more than six to eight people, so everyone gets the chance to speak up.

Let us consider how we may spur one another on toward love and good deeds. Let us not give up meeting together, as some are in the habit of doing, but let us encourage one another. Hebrews 10:24–25

Private Coaching

You may meet with your small-group coach—or another coach—for private coaching by phone or in person. A coach helps you develop a career path, solve current job problems, prepare your résumé, or guide your search.

Many members develop long-term relation-ships with their coaches to get advice throughout their careers. If you are paying for the coaching yourself (as opposed to having your employer pay), please pay the coach directly (charges vary from $100 to $175 per hour). **Private coaching is *not* included in The Five O'Clock Club seminar or membership fee.** For coach matching, see our website or call **1-800-575-3587** (or **212-286-4500** in New York).

From the Club History, Written in the 1890s

At The Five O'Clock Club, [people] of all shades of political belief—as might be said of all trades and creeds—have met together. . . . The variety continues almost to a monotony. . . . [The Club's] good fellowship and geniality—not to say hospitality—has reached them all.

It has been remarked of clubs that they serve to level rank. If that were possible in this country, it would probably be true, if leveling rank means the appreciation of people of equal abilities as equals; but in The Five O'Clock Club it has been a most gratifying and noteworthy fact that no lines have ever been drawn save those which are essential to the honor and good name of any association. Strangers are invited by the club or by any members, [as gentlepeople], irrespective of aristocracy, plutocracy or occupation, and are so treated always. Nor does the thought of a [person's] social position ever enter into the meetings. People of wealth and people of moderate means sit side by side, finding in each other much to praise and admire and little to justify snarlishness or adverse criticism. People meet as people—not as the representatives of a set—and having so met, dwell not in worlds of envy or distrust, but in union and collegiality, forming kindly thoughts of each other in their heart of hearts.

In its methods, The Five O'Clock Club is plain, easy-going and unconventional. It has its "isms" and some peculiarities of procedure, but simplicity characterizes them all. The sense of propriety, rather than rules of order, governs its meetings, and that informality which carries with it sincerity of motive and spontaneity of effort, prevails within it. Its very name indicates informality, and, indeed, one of the reasons said to have induced its adoption was the fact that members or guests need not don their dress suits to attend the meetings, if they so desired. This informality, however, must be distinguished from the informality of Bohemian-ism. For The Five O'Clock Club, informality, above convenience, means sobriety, refinement of thought and speech, good breeding and good order. To this sort of informality much of its success is due.

Fortune, The New York Times, Black Enterprise, Business Week, NPR, CNBC and ABC-TV are some of the places you've seen, heard, or read about us.

The Schedule

See our website for the specific dates for each topic. All groups use a similar schedule in each time zone.

Fee: $49 annual membership (includes Beginners Kit, subscription to *The Five O'Clock News,* and access to the Members Only section of our website), **plus** session fees based on member's income (price for the Insider Program includes audio-CD lectures, which retails for $150).

Reservations required for first session. Unused sessions are transferable to anyone you choose or can be donated to members attending more than 16 sessions who are having financial difficulty.

The Five O'Clock Club's programs are geared to recent graduates, professionals, managers, and executives from a wide variety of industries and professions. Most earn from $30,000 to $400,000 per year. Half the members are employed; half are unemployed. *You will be in a group of your peers.*

To register, please fill out form on the web (at www.fiveoclockclub.com)
or call 1-800-575-3587 (or 212-286-4500 in New York).

Lecture Presentation Schedule

- History of the 5OCC
- The 5OCC Approach to Job Search
- Developing New Targets for Your Search
- Two-Minute Pitch: Keystone of Your Search
- Using Research and Internet for Your Search
- The Keys to Effective Networking
- Getting the Most Out of Your Contacts
- Getting Interviews: Direct/Targeted Mail
- Beat the Odds When Using Search Firms and Ads
- Developing New Momentum in Your Search
- The 5OCC Approach to Interviewing
- Advanced Interviewing Techniques
- How to Handle Difficult Interview Questions
- How to Turn Job Interviews into Offers

- Successful Job Hunter's Report
- Four-Step Salary-Negotiation Method

All groups run continuously. Dates are posted on our website. The textbooks used by all members of The Five O'Clock Club may be ordered on our website or purchased at major bookstores.

The original Five O'Clock Club was formed in Philadelphia in 1883. It was made up of the leaders of the day who shared their experiences "in a spirit of fellowship and good humor."

Questions You May Have About The Weekly Job-search Strategy Group

Job hunters are not always the best judges of what they need during a search. For example, most are interested in lectures on answering ads on the Internet or working with search firms. We cover those topics, but strategically they are relatively unimportant in an effective job search.

At The Five O'Clock Club, you get the information you really need in your search—*such as how to target more effectively, how to get more interviews, and how to turn job interviews into offers.* What's more, you will work in a small group with the best coaches in the business. In these strategy sessions, your group will help you decide what to do, this week and every week, to move your search along. You will learn by being coached and by coaching others in your group.

> *We find ourselves not independently of other people and institutions but through them. We never get to the bottom of our selves on our own. We discover who we are face to face and side by side with others in work, love, and learning.* —Robert N. Bellah, et al., *Habits of the Heart*

Here are a few other points:

- For best results, attend on a regular basis. Your group gets to know you and will coach you to eliminate whatever you may be doing wrong—or refine what you are doing right.
- The Five O'Clock Club is a members-only organization. To get started in the small-group teleconference sessions, you must purchase a minimum of 10 sessions.
- The teleconference sessions include the set of 16 audio-CD presentations on Five O'Clock Club methodology. In-person groups do not include CDs.
- After that, you may purchase blocks of 5 or 10 sessions.
- We sell multiple sessions to make administration easier.
- If you miss a session, you may make it up any time. You may even transfer unused time to a friend.
- Although many people find jobs quickly (even people who have been unemployed a long time), others have more difficult searches. Plan to be in it for the long haul and you'll do better.
- Carefully read all of the material in this section. It will help you decide whether or not to attend.
- The first week, pay attention to the strategies used by the others in your group. Soak up all the information you can.
- Read the books before you come in the second week. They will help you move your search along.

To register:

1. Read this section and fill out the application.
2. After you become a member and get your Beginners Kit, call to reserve a space for the first time you attend.

To assign you to a career coach, we need to know:

- your current (or last) field or industry
- the kind of job you would like next (if you know)
- your desired salary range in general terms

For private coaching, we suggest you attend the small group and ask to see your group leader to give you continuity.

The Five O'Clock Club is plain, easy-going and unconventional. . . . Members or guests need not don their dress suits to attend the meetings. (From the Club History, written in the 1890s)

What Happens at the Meetings?

Each week, job searchers from various industries and professions meet in small groups. The groups specialize in professionals, managers, executives, or recent college graduates. Usually, half are employed and half are unemployed.

The weekly program is in two parts. First, there is a lecture on some aspect of The Five O'Clock Club methodology. Then, job hunters meet in small groups headed by senior full-time professional career coaches.

The first week, get the textbooks, listen to the lecture, and get assigned to your small group. During your first session, *listen* to the others in your group. You learn a lot by listening to how your peers are strategizing *their* searches.

By the second week, you will have read the materials. Now we can start to work on *your* search strategy and help *you* decide what to do next to move your search along. For example, we'll help you figure out how to get more inter-views in your target area or how to turn inter-views into job offers.

In the third week, you will see major progress made by other members of your group and you may notice major progress in your own search as well.

By the third or fourth week, most members are conducting full and effective searches. Over the remaining weeks, you will tend to keep up a full search rather than go after only one or two leads. You will regularly aim to have 6 to 10 things *in the works* at all times. These will generally be in specific target areas you have identified, will keep your search on target, and will increase your chances of getting multiple job offers from which to choose.

Those who stick with the process find it works.

Some people prefer to just listen for a few weeks before they start their job search and that's okay, too.

How Much Does It Cost?

It is against the policy of The Five O'Clock Club to charge individuals heavy up-front fees. Our competitors charge $4,000 to $6,000 or more, up front. Our average fee is $360 for 10 sessions (which includes audio CDs of 16 presentations for those in the teleconference program). Executives pay an average of $810 for 10 sessions. For administrative reasons, we charge for 5 or 10 additional sessions at a time.

You must have the books so you can begin studying them before the second session. (You can purchase them on our website or at major bookstores.) If you don't do the homework, you will tend to waste the time of others in the group by asking questions covered in the texts.

Is the Small Group Right for Me?

The Five O'Clock Club process is for you if:

- You are truly interested in job hunting.
- You have *some* idea of the kind of job you want.
- You are a professional, manager, or executive—or want to be.
- You want to participate in a group process on a regular basis.
- You realize that finding or changing jobs and careers is hard work, but you are absolutely willing and able to do it.

If you have no idea about the kind of job you want next, you may attend one or two group sessions to start. *Then* see a *coach privately* for one or two sessions, develop tentative job targets, and return to the group. You may work with your small-group coach or contact us through our website or by calling **1-800-575-3587** (or **212-286-4500** in New York) for referral to another coach.

How Long Will It Take Me to Get a Job?

Although our members tend to be from fields or industries where they expect to have difficult searches, *the average person who attends regularly finds a new position within 10 sessions.* Some take less time and others take more.

One thing we know for sure: **Research shows that those who get *regular* coaching during their searches get jobs faster and at higher rates of pay than those who search on their own or simply take a course.** This makes sense. If a person comes only when they think they have a problem, they are usually wrong. They probably had a problem a few weeks ago but didn't realize it. Or the problem may be dif-ferent from the one they thought they had. Those who come regularly benefit from the observations others make about their searches. Problems are solved before they become severe or are prevented altogether.

Those who attend regularly also learn a lot by paying attention and helping others in the group. This *secondhand* learning can shorten your search by weeks. When you hear the problems of others who are ahead of you in the search, you can avoid them completely. People in your group will come to know you and will point out subtleties you may not have noticed that interviewers will never tell you.

Will I Be with Others from My Field/Industry?

Probably, but it's not that important. You will learn a lot and have a much more creative search if you are in a group of people who are in your general salary range but not exactly like you. Our clients are from virtually every field and industry. The *process* is what will help you.

We've been doing this since 1978 and under-stand your needs. That's why the mix we provide is the best you can get.

Career Coaching Firms Charge $4,000–$6,000 Up Front. How Can You Charge Such a Small Fee?

1. We have no advertising costs, because 90 per-cent of those who attend have been referred by other members.

A hefty up-front fee would bind you to us, but we have been more successful by treating people ethically and having them pretty much *pay as they go.*

We need a certain number of people to cover expenses. When lots of people get jobs quickly and leave us, we could go into the red. But as long as members refer others, we will continue to provide this service at a fair price.

2. We focus strictly on *job-search strategy,* and encourage our clients to attend free support groups if they need emotional support. We focus on getting *jobs,* which reduces the time clients spend with us and the amount they pay.

3. We attract the best coaches, and our clients make more progress per session than they would elsewhere, which also reduces their costs.

4. We have expert administrators and a sophisticated computer system that reduces our over-head and increases our ability to track your progress.

May I Change Coaches?

Yes. Great care is taken in assigning you to your initial coach. However, if you want to change once for any reason, you may do it. We don't encourage group hopping: It is better for you to stick with a group so that everyone gets to know you. On the other hand, we want you to feel comfortable. So if you tell us you prefer a different group, you will be transferred immediately.

What If I Have a Quick Question Outside of the Group Session?

Some people prefer to see their group coach privately. Others prefer to meet with a different coach to get another point of view. Whatever you decide, remember that the group fee does *not* cover coaching time outside the group session. Therefore, if you wanted to speak with a coach between sessions—even for *quick questions*—you would normally meet with the coach first for a private session so he or she can get to know you better. *Easy, quick questions* are usually more complicated than they appear. After your first private session, some coaches will allow you to pay in advance for one hour of coaching time, which you can then use for quick questions by phone (usually a 15-minute minimum is charged). Since each coach has an individual way of operating, find out how the coach arranges these things.

What If I Want to Start My Own Business?

The process of becoming a consultant is essentially the same as job hunting and lots of consultants attend Five O'Clock Club meetings. However, if you want to buy a franchise or existing business or start a growth business, you should see a private coach.

How Can I Be Sure That The Five O'Clock Club Small-Group Sessions Will Be Right for Me?

Before you actually participate in any of the small-group sessions, you can get an idea of the quality of our service by listening to all 16 audio CDs that you purchased. If you are dissatisfied with the CDs for any reason, return the package within 30 days for a full refund.

Whatever you decide, just remember: *It has been proven that those who receive regular help during their searches get jobs faster and at higher rates of pay than those who search on their own or simply attend a course.* If you get a job just one or two weeks faster because of this program, it will have more than paid for itself. And you may *transfer unused sessions to anyone you choose.* However, the person you choose must be or become a member.

When Your Employer Pays

Does your employer care about you and others whom they ask to leave the organization? If so, ask them to consider The Five O'Clock Club for your outplacement help. The Five O'Clock Club puts you and your job search first, offering a career-coaching program of the highest quality at the lowest possible price to your employer.

Over 25 Years of Research

The Five O'Clock Club was started in 1978 as a research-based organization. Job hunters tried various techniques and reported their results back to the group. We developed a variety of guidelines so job hunters could choose the techniques best for them.

The methodology was tested and refined on professionals, managers, and executives (and those aspiring to be) from all occupations. Annual salaries ranged from $30,000 to $400,000; 50 per-cent were employed and 50 percent were unemployed.

Since its beginning, The Five O'Clock Club has tracked trends. Over time, our advice has changed as the job market has changed. What worked in the past is insufficient for today's job market. Today's Five O'Clock Club promotes all our relevant original strategies—and so much more.

As an employee-advocacy organization, The Five O'Clock Club focuses on providing the services and information that the job hunter needs most.

Get the Help You Need Most: 100 Percent Coaching

There's a myth in outplacement circles that a terminated employee just needs a desk, a phone, and minimal career coaching. *Our experience clearly shows that downsized workers need qualified, reliable coaching more than any-thing else.*

Most traditional outplacement packages last only 3 months. The average executive gets office space and only 5 hours of career coaching during this time. Yet the service job hunters need most is the career coaching itself—not a desk and a phone.

Most professionals, managers, and executives are right in the thick of negotiations with prospective employers at the 3-month mark. Yet that is precisely when traditional outplacement ends, leaving job hunters stranded and sometimes ruining deals.

It is astonishing how often job hunters and employers alike are impressed by the databases of *job postings* claimed by outplacement firms. Yet only 10 percent of all jobs are filled through ads and another 10 percent are filled through search firms. Instead, direct contact and networking—done The Five O'Clock Club way—are more effective for most searches.

You Get a Safety Net

Imagine getting a package that protects you for a full year or more. Imagine knowing you can comeback if your new job doesn't work out—even months later. Imagine trying consulting work if you like. If you later decide it's not for you, you can come back to The Five O'Clock Club.

We can offer you a safety net of one full year's career coaching because our method is so effective that few people actually need more than 10 weeks in our proven program. But you're protected for a year.

You'll Job Search with Those Who Are Employed—How Novel!

Let's face it. It can be depressing to spend your days at an outplacement firm where everyone is unemployed. At The Five O'Clock Club, half the attendees are working, and this makes the atmosphere cheerier and helps to move your search along.

What's more, you'll be in a small group of your peers, all of whom are using The Five O'Clock Club method. Our research proves that those who attend the small group regularly and use The Five O'Clock Club methods get jobs faster and at higher rates of pay than those who only work privately with a career coach through-out their searches.

So Many Poor Attempts

Nothing is sadder than meeting someone who has already been getting job-search *help,* but the wrong kind. They've learned the traditional techniques that are no longer effective. Most have poor résumés and inappropriate targets and don't know how to turn job interviews into offers.

You'll Get Quite a Package

You'll get at least 14 hours of private coaching—well in excess of what you would get at a traditional outplacement firm. You may even want to use a few hours after you start your new job.

And you get up to one full year of small-group career coaching. In addition, you get books, audio CDs, and other helpful materials.

To Get Started

The day your human resources manager calls us authorizing Five O'Clock Club outplacement, we will immediately ship you the books, CDs, and other materials and assign you to a private coach and a small group.

Then we'll monitor your search. Frankly, we care about you more than we care about your employer. And since your employer cares about you, they're glad we feel this way—because they know we'll take care of you.

What They Say about Us

The Five O'Clock Club product is much better, far more useful than my outplacement package. —Senior executive and Five O'Clock Club member

The Club kept the juices flowing. You're told what to do, what not to do. There were fresh ideas. I went through an outplacement service that, frankly, did not help. If they had done as much as the Five O'Clock Club did, I would have landed sooner. —Another member

When Your *Employer* Pays for The Five O'Clock Club, *You* Get:

- **Up to 40 hours of guaranteed private career coaching** to determine a career direction, develop a résumé, plan salary negotiations, and so on. In fact, if you need a second opinion during your search, we can arrange that too.
- **ONE YEAR (or more) of small-group teleconference coaching** (average about 5 or 6 participants in a group) headed by a senior Five O'Clock Club career consultant. That way, if you lose your next job, you can come back. Or if you want to try consulting work and then decide you **don't like it, you can come back.**
- **Two-year membership** in The Five O'Clock Club: Beginners Kit and two-year subscription to *The Five O'Clock News*.
- **The complete set of our four books** for professionals, managers, and executives who are in job search.
- **A boxed set of 16 audio CDs** of Five O'Clock Club presentations.

COMPARISON OF EMPLOYER-PAID PACKAGES

Typical Package	Traditional Outplacement	The Five O'Clock Club
Who is the client?	The organization	Job hunters. We are employee advocates. We always do what is in the best interest of job hunters.
The clientele	All are unemployed	Half of our attendees are unemployed; half are employed. There is an upbeat atmosphere; networking is enhanced.
Length/type of service	3 months, primarily office space	1 year, exclusively career coaching
Service ends	After 3 months—or before if the client lands a job or consulting	After 1 full year, no matter what. You can return if you lose your next job, if your assignment ends, or if you need advice after starting your new job.
Small-group coaching	Sporadic for 3 months; Coach varies	Every week for up to 1 year; same coach
Private coaching	Coach varies	14 (or more) hours guaranteed (depending on level of service purchased)
Support materials	Generic manual	• 4 textbooks based on over 25 years of job-search research • Sixteen 40-minute lectures on audio CDs • Beginners Kit of search information • 2-year subscription to the Five O'Clock Club magazine, devoted to career-management articles
Facilities	Cubicle, phone, computer access	None; use home phone and computer

The Way We Are

The Five O'Clock Club means sobriety, refinement of thought and speech, good breeding and good order. To this, much of its success is due. The Five O'Clock Club is easy-going and unconventional. A sense of propriety, rather than rules of order, governs its meetings.
  —J. Hampton Moore, *History of The Five O'Clock Club* (written in the 1890s)

Just like the members of the original Five O'Clock Club, today's members want an ongoing relationship. George Vaillant, in his seminal work on successful people, found that "what makes or breaks our luck seems to be . . . our sustained relationships with other people." (George E.Vaillant, *Adaptation to Life,* Harvard University Press, 1995)

Five O'Clock Club members know that much of the program's benefit comes from simply showing up. Showing up will encourage you to do what you need to do when you are not here. And over the course of several weeks, certain things will become evident that are not evident now.

Five O'Clock Club members learn from each other: The group leader is not the only one with answers. The leader brings factual information to the meetings and keeps the discussion in line. But the answers to some problems may lie within you or with others in the group.

Five O'Clock Club members encourage each other. They listen, see similarities with their own situations, and learn from that. And they listen to see how they may help others. You may come across information or a contact that could help someone else in the group. Passing on that information is what we're all about.

If you are a new member here, listen to others to learn the process. And read the books so you will know the basics that others already know. When everyone understands the basics, this keeps the meetings on a high level, interesting, and helpful to everyone.

Five O'Clock Club members are in this together, but they know that ultimately they are each responsible for solving their own problems with God's help. Take the time to learn the process, and you will become better at analyzing your own situation, as well as the situations of others. You will be learning a method that will serve you the rest of your life, and in areas of your life apart from your career.

Five O'Clock Club members are kind to each other. They control their frustrations because venting helps no one. Because many may be stressed, be kind and go the extra length to keep this place calm and happy. It is your respite from the world outside and a place for you to find comfort and FUN. Relax and enjoy yourself, learn what you can, and help where you can. And have a ball doing it.

There arises from the hearts of busy [people] a love of variety, a yearning for relaxation of thought as well as of body, and a craving for a generous and spontaneous fraternity. —J. Hampton Moore, *History of The Five O'Clock Club*

Lexicon Used At The Five O'Clock Club

Use The Five O'Clock Club lexicon as a shorthand to express where you are in your job search. It will focus you and those in your group.

I. Overview and Assessment

How many hours a week are you spending on your search?
Spend 35 hours on a full-time search, 15 hours on a part-time search.

What are your job targets?
Tell the group. A target includes industry or company size, position, and geographic area. The group can help assess how good your targets are. Take a look at *Measuring Your Targets*.

How does your résumé position you?
The summary and body should make you look appropriate to your target.

What are your backup targets?
Decide at the beginning of the search before the first campaign. Then you won't get stuck.

Have you done the Assessment?
If your targets are wrong, everything is wrong. (Do the Assessment in *Targeting a Great Career.*) Or a counselor can help you privately to deter-mine possible job targets.

II. Getting Interviews

How large is your target (e.g., 30 companies)?

How many of them have you contacted?

Contact them all.

How can you get (more) leads?

You will not get a job through search firms, ads, networking, or direct contact. Those are techniques for getting interviews—job leads. Use the right terminology, especially after a person gets a job. Do not say, "How did you get the job?" if you really want to know "Where did you get the lead for that job?"

Do you have 6 to 10 things in the works?

You may want the group to help you land one job. After they help you with your strategy, they should ask, "How many other things do you have in the works?" If *none,* the group can brainstorm how you can get more things going: through search firms, ads, networking, or direct contact. Then you are more likely to turn the job you want into an offer because you will seem more valuable. What's more, 5 will fall away through no fault of your own. Don't go after only 1 job.

How's your Two-Minute Pitch?

Practice a *tailored* Two-Minute Pitch. Tell the group the job title and industry of the hiring manager they should pretend they are for a role-playing exercise. You will be surprised how good the group is at critiquing pitches. (Practice a few weeks in a row.) Use your pitch to separate you from your competition.

You seem to be in Stage One (or Stage Two or Stage Three) of your search.

Know where you are. This is the key measure of your search.

Are you seen as an insider or an outsider?

See *How to Change Careers* for becoming an insider. If people are saying, "I wish I had an opening for someone like you," you are doing well in meetings. If the industry is strong, then it's only a matter of time before you get a job.

III. Turning Interviews into Offers

Do you want this job?

If you do not want the job, perhaps you want an offer, if only for practice. If you are not willing to go for it, the group's suggestions will not work.

Who are your likely competitors and how can you outshine and outlast them?

You will not get a job simply because "they liked me." The issues are deeper. Ask the interviewer: "Where are you in the hiring process? What kind of person would be your ideal candidate? How do I stack up?"

What are your next steps?

What are *you* planning to do if the hiring manager doesn't call by a certain date or what are you planning to do to assure that the hiring manager *does* call you?

Can you prove you can do the job?

Don't just take the *trust me* approach. Consider your competition.

Which job positions you best for the long run? Which job is the best fit?

Don't decide only on the basis of salary. You will most likely have another job after this. See which job looks best on your résumé and will make you stronger for the next time. In addition, find a fit for your personality. If you don't *fit*, it is unlikely you will do well there. The group can help you turn interviews into offers and give you feedback on which job is best for you.

> *"Believe me, with self-examination and a lot of hard work with our coaches, you can find the job . . . you can have the career . . . you can live the life you've always wanted!"*
>
> Sincerely,
> Kate Wendleton

Membership

As a member of The Five O'Clock Club, you get:

- A year's subscription to *The Five O'Clock News*—10 issues filled with information on career development and job-search techniques, focusing on the experiences of real people.
- Access to *reasonably priced* weekly seminars featuring individualized attention to your specific needs in small groups supervised by our senior coaches.
- Access to one-on-one coaching to help you answer specific questions, solve current job problems, prepare your résumé, or take an in-depth look at your career path. You choose the coach and pay the coach directly.
- An attractive Beginners Kit containing information based on over 25 years of research on who gets jobs . . . and why . . . that will enable you to improve your job-search techniques—immediately!

- The opportunity to exchange ideas and experiences with other job searchers and career changers.

All that access, all that information, all that expertise for the annual membership fee of only $49, plus seminar fees.

How to become a member—by mail or E-mail:

Send your name, address, phone number, how you heard about us, and your check for $49 (made payable to "The Five O'Clock Club") to The Five O'Clock Club, 300 East 40th Street—Suite 6L, New York, NY 10016, or sign up at www.fiveoclockclub.com.

We will immediately mail you a Five O'Clock Club Membership Card, the Beginners Kit, and information on our seminars followed by our magazine. Then, call 1-800-575-3587 (or 212-286-4500 in New York) or e-mail us (at info@fiveoclockclub.com) to:

- reserve a space for the first time you plan to attend, or
- be matched with a Five O'Clock Club coach.

Membership Application

The Five O'Clock Club

____Yes! I want to become a member!

I want access to the most effective methods for finding jobs, as well as for developing and managing my career.

I enclose my check for $49 for 1 year; $75 for 2 years—payable to The Five O'Clock Club. I will receive a Beginners Kit, a subscription to *The Five O'Clock News*, access to the Members Only area on our website, and a network of career coaches. Reasonably priced seminars are held across the country.

Name: _____

Address: _____

City: State: Zip:_____

Work phone: (____)_____

Home phone: (____)_____

E-mail: _____

Date: _____

How I heard about the Club: _____

For Executives Only (Applying Business Techniques to Your Job Search)
The following optional information is for statistical purposes. Thanks for your help.
Salary range:
___$100,000 to $200,000   ___$200,000 to $300,000   ___$300,000 and above
Age: __ 30–39 __ 40–49 __ 50+
Gender: __ Male __ Female
Current or most recent position/title: _____

Please send to:
Membership Director, The Five O'Clock Club,
300 East 40th St., Suite 6L, New York, NY 10016

The original Five O'Clock Club® was formed in Philadelphia in 1893. It was made up of the leaders of the day who shared their experiences "in a setting of fellowship and good humor."

Index

About the Authors

BILL BELKNAP has thirty years of senior management and human resources experience, with more than 10 years at the Vice President level. He has headed the human resource function for fast-paced companies in a variety of industries, including high tech, medical cost containment, consumer products, office products and financial information.

A unique aspect of Bill's background: he was a successful sales rep and sales manager at Xerox before starting his human resources career so he brings a strong business perspective to his coaching. Fourteen years ago he co-founded a management-consulting firm, where he directs its Human Resources practice. The firm's clients have included an array of industries from CRM software to cosmetics and financial services.

His areas of expertise include executive and career coaching, employee selection and retention, executive recruiting, and management training.

Bill has been a certified Five O'Clock Club Guild coach since 2002. He works primarily with executive clients.

On the personal side, Bill is an amateur magician and fitness enthusiast. He recently completed his twenty-first triathlon. He is a graduate of Denison University.

HÉLÈNE SEILER has twenty years of international consulting and human resource management experience. She has been a certified Five O'Clock Club Guild coach since 2003.

Since 1997 she has lead a boutique career management company focused on international executives' search and coaching. Prior to that, Hélène worked as a change management and strategy consultant in Western Europe and in North America. She coaches in English and in French.

Through coaching and training sessions, she assists European and North American corporations with executives' talent management and leadership development, including assessment, career management, recruiting, on-boarding and outplacement. She also works privately with executives through their job search process.

Hélène Seiler holds a Master of Management Science from HEC School of Management. She is a Professional Certified Coach with The International Coaches Federation, and is an adjunct coach for the Center of Creative Leadership.

Hélène is a French and Swiss national and a permanent US resident. An active community leader, she coordinates US alumni career services for her alma mater. An amateur musician, she manages a town-wide classical music program for elementary school children. A passionate mountain hiker, she has climbed about a half a dozen summits worldwide, most recently Mount Kilimanjaro.

She lives in Connecticut with her husband and two children.

About the Five O'Clock Club and the "Fruytagie" Canvas

Five O'Clock Club members are special. We attract upbeat, ambitious, dynamic, intelligent people—and that makes it fun for all of us. Most of our members are professionals, managers, executives, consultants, and freelancers. We also include recent college graduates and those aiming to get into the professional ranks, as well as people in their 40s, 50s, and even 60s. Most members' salaries range from $30,000 to $400,000 (one-third of our members earn in excess of $100,000 a year). For those who cannot attend a Club, *The Five O'Clock Club Book Series* contains all of our methodologies—and our spirit.

The Philosophy of The Five O'Clock Club

The "Fruytagie" Canvas by Patricia Kelly, depicted here, symbolizes our philosophy. The original, which is actually 52.5 by 69 inches, hangs in the offices of The Five O'Clock Club in Manhattan. It is reminiscent of popular 16th century Dutch "fruytagie," or fruit tapestries, which depicted abundance and prosperity.

I was attracted to this piece because it seemed to fit the spirit of our people at The Five O'Clock Club. This was confirmed when the artist, who was not aware of what I did for a living, added these words to the canvas: "The gar-den is abundant, prosperous and magical." Later, it took me only 10 minutes to write the blank verse "The Garden of

Life," because it came from my heart. The verse reflects our philosophy and describes the kind of people who are members of the Club.

I'm always inspired by Five O'Clock Clubbers. They show others the way through their quiet behavior . . . their kindness . . . their generosity . . . their hard work . . . under God's care.

We share what we have with others. We are in this lush, exciting place together—with our brothers and sisters—and reach out for harmony. The garden is abundant. The job market is exciting. And Five O'Clock Clubbers believe that there is enough for everyone.

About the Artist's Method

To create her tapestry-like art, Kelly developed a unique style of stenciling. She hand-draws and hand-cuts each stencil, both in the negative and positive for each image. Her elaborate technique also includes a lengthy multilayering process incorporating Dutch metal leaves and gilding, numerous transparent glazes, paints, and wax pencils.

Kelly also paints the back side of the canvas using multiple washes of reds, violets, and golds. She uses this technique to create a heavy vibration of color, which in turn reflects the color onto the surface of the wall against which the canvas hangs.

The canvas is suspended by a heavy braided silk cord threaded into large brass grommets inserted along the top. Like a tapestry, the hemmed canvas is attached to a gold-gilded dowel with finials. The entire work is hung from a sculpted wall ornament.

Our staff is inspired every day by the tapestry and by the members of The Five O'Clock Club. We all work hard—and have FUN! The garden *is* abundant—with enough for everyone. We wish you lots of success in your career. We—and your fellow members of The Five O'Clock Club—will work with you on it.

—Kate Wendleton, President

The original Five O'Clock Club was formed in Philadelphia in 1883. It was made up of the leaders of the day, who shared their experiences "in a spirit of fellowship and good humor."

 **THE GARDEN OF LIFE IS** abundant, prosperous and magical. ❦ In this garden, there is enough for everyone. ❦ Share the fruit and the knowledge ❦ Our brothers and we are in this lush, exciting place together. ❦ Let's show others the way. ❦ Kindness. Generosity. ❦ Hard work. ❦ God's care.